The Open University

The
Molecular World

Book 1
A Prologue to the Course

Lesley Smart

Book 2
Introducing the Molecular World

David Johnson

The Open University,
Walton Hall,
Milton Keynes,
MK7 6AA

1 2777919

First published 2002

Edited, designed and typeset by The Open University.

Printed in the United Kingdom by Bath Press.

ISBN 0 7492 97549

This publication forms part of an Open University course, S205 *The Molecular World*. The complete list of texts which make up this course can be found on the back cover. Details of this and other Open University courses can be obtained from the Call Centre, PO Box 724, The Open University, Milton Keynes MK7 6ZS, United Kingdom: tel. +44 (0)1908 653231, e-mail ces-gen@open.ac.uk

Alternatively, you may visit the Open University website at http://www.open.ac.uk where you can learn more about the wide range of courses and packs offered at all levels by The Open University.

To purchase this publication or other components of Open University courses, contact Open University Worldwide Ltd, The Open University, Walton Hall, Milton Keynes MK7 6AA, United Kingdom:
tel. +44 (0)1908 858785; fax +44 (0)1908 858787; e-mail ouwenq@open.ac.uk; website http://www.ouw.co.uk

1.1

The Molecular World Course Team

Course Team Chair
Lesley Smart

Open University Authors
Eleanor Crabb (Book 8)
Adrian Dobbs (Book 10)
Michael Gagan (Book 3, Book 7)
Charles Harding (Book 9)
Rob Janes (Book 9)
David Johnson (Book 1, Book 2, Book 4, Book 9)
Elaine Moore (Book 6)
Michael Mortimer (Book 5)
Lesley Smart (Book 1, Book 3, Book 8)
Peter Taylor (Book 5, Book 7, Book 10)
Judy Thomas (*Study File*)
Ruth Williams (skills, assessment questions)
Other authors whose previous contributions to the earlier
courses S246 and S247 have been invaluable in the
preparation of this course: Tim Allott, Alan Bassindale, Stuart
Bennett, Keith Bolton, John Coyle, John Emsley, Jim Iley, Ray
Jones, Joan Mason, Peter Morrod, Jane Nelson, Malcolm
Rose, Richard Taylor, Kiki Warr.

Course Manager
Mike Bullivant

Course Team Assistant
Debbie Gingell

Course Editors
Ian Nuttall
Bina Sharma
Peter Twomey

CD-ROM Production
Andrew Bertie
Greg Black
Matthew Brown
Philip Butcher
Chris Denham
Spencer Harben
David Palmer

BBC
Rosalind Bain
Stephen Haggard
Melanie Heath
Darren Wycherley
Tim Martin
Jessica Barrington

Course Reader
Cliff Ludman

Course Assessor
Professor Eddie Abel, University of Exeter

Audio and Audiovisual recording
Kirsten Hintner
Andrew Rix

Design
Steve Best
Carl Gibbard
Sarah Hack
Mike Levers
Sian Lewis
John Taylor
Howie Twiner

Library
Judy Thomas

Picture Researchers
Lydia Eaton
Deana Plummer

Technical Assistance
Brandon Cook
Pravin Patel

Consultant Authors
Ronald Dell (*Case Study:* Batteries and Fuel Cells)
Chris Falshaw (Book 10)
Andrew Galwey (*Case Study:* Acid Rain)
Guy Grant (*Case Study:* Molecular Modelling)
Alan Heaton (*Case Study:* Industrial Organic Chemistry,
     Case Study: Industrial Inorganic Chemistry)
Bob Hill (*Case Study:* Polymers and Gels)
Roger Hill (Book 10)
Anya Hunt (*Case Study:* Forensic Science)
Corrie Imrie (*Case Study:* Liquid Crystals)
Clive McKee (Book 5)
Bob Murray (*Study File*, Book 11)
Andrew Platt (*Case Study:* Forensic Science)
Ray Wallace (*Study File*, Book 11)
Craig Williams (*Case Study:* Zeolites)

The atomic theory has triumphed.
One by one the many sceptics drop away,
withdrawing their objections that were, for so long,
both legitimate and useful.

Jean Baptiste Perrin
winner of the Nobel Prize for Physics 1926

BOOK 1
A PROLOGUE TO THE COURSE

CONTENTS

INTRODUCTION

Welcome to S205 *The Molecular World*. Understanding molecules, their shape, structure and how they are made, is the linchpin for all the sciences: molecules are what we are made of, what we eat and drink, and what much of the world around us is composed of. Molecules are the messengers in the body, and even the thought processes of the brain require the production and transfer of molecules. Molecules are made up of atoms bonded together in different combinations, and can vary in size from the simplest diatomic molecules, such as the oxygen (Figure 1.1) and nitrogen in the air, which have only two atoms each, to large biological molecules, such as proteins and enzymes, which have many thousands of atoms (Figure 1.2). If we think of the extended structures that we find in some rocks (such as quartz or diamond) as a single molecule bounded only by the size of the specimen, then these giant molecules contain literally billions of atoms (Figure 1.3).

The Books in this Course will introduce you to the huge variety of molecules that you experience in your everyday lives — probably without even realizing it — for almost everything that you see, touch, smell and taste, is composed of different molecules (Figure 1.4); even what you hear is caused by the sudden movement of the molecules in the air due to changes in pressure as we speak! We shall introduce you to the shapes and structures of the simplest and the most complex molecules, and discuss how we can determine their structures and shapes; you will be able to view 3-D models of many of these molecules (Figure 1.5) using a program on a CD-ROM* which allows you to move them around, view them from any direction, and even to highlight useful features such as the α-helices and β-sheets in the structures of proteins (Figure 1.2b). We shall explore how molecules are held together by different types of bonding, how they interact with one another to create new molecules, and the rates at which they do it.

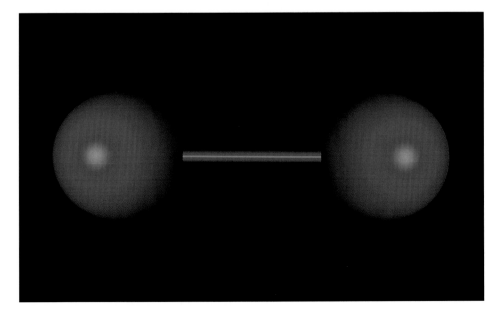

Figure 1.1
A molecule of oxygen, O_2. ⌨

* Molecules marked with a computer symbol can be viewed using WebLab ViewerLite™ from the CD-ROM accompanying this Book (see Section 11.1.3).

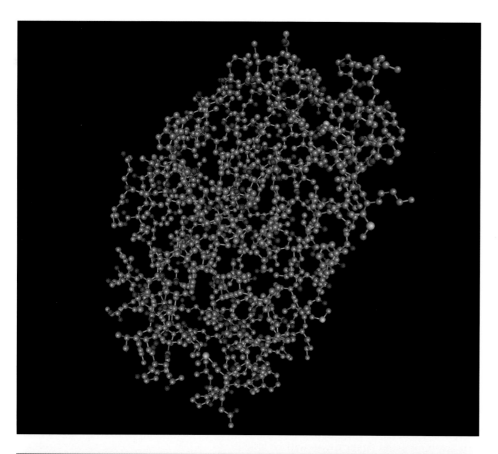

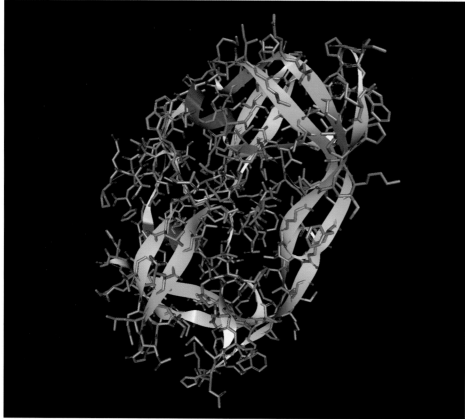

Figure 1.2
Two representations of
HIVprotease1 using WebLab
ViewerLite.

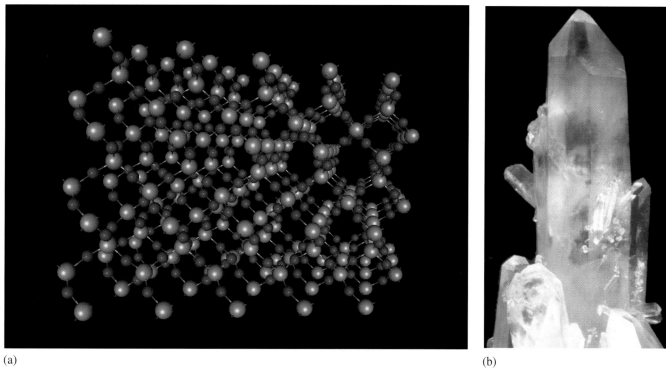

(a)

(b)

Figure 1.3 (a) The structure of quartz; (b) a crystal of quartz. 💻

Figure 1.4 The distinctive smell of garlic is due to a particular molecule, namely 2-propenyl disulfide.

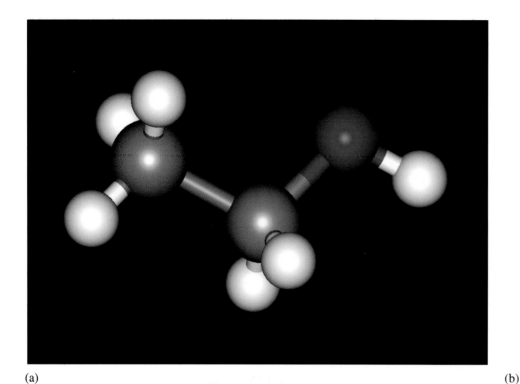

(a)

(b)

$$H-\underset{\underset{H}{|}}{\overset{\overset{H}{|}}{C}}-\underset{\underset{H}{|}}{\overset{\overset{H}{|}}{C}}-OH$$

(c)

Figure 1.5
(a) A 'ball and stick' representation of ethanol (the 'alcohol' found in wines and spirits), which shows the positions of the atoms and the bonds joining them; (b) the formula of ethanol; (c) a 'space-filling' representation of ethanol with a more realistic view of the sizes of the electron clouds around each atom. 💻

Chemistry is the scientific discipline that studies the structure and interactions of molecules, so this introduction is a good place to explore the role of chemistry in the modern world. Chemistry has held a pivotal role in the sciences throughout history, and continues to do so. For example, it has brought us the medicines that have both extended and improved the quality of so many people's lives — antibiotics, steroids, anti-cancer drugs, to name but a few. Looking around you, notice the many synthetic materials that have been developed in recent years: polymers, plastics, synthetic fabrics, non-stick surfaces, strong alloys. Much of the electrical equipment in your house will be powered by batteries, and the development of new lightweight batteries have made portable cellular phones and laptop computers possible. The displays on electrical goods — clocks, calculators, mobile phones — use liquid crystals. All of these developments have been made by chemists. Photography, film, video and sound recording have all relied on chemists to discover and provide the sensitive recording materials. And the list could go on. The chemical industry plays a very important part in the national economy, and covers a vast range from oil-refining and the petrochemical industry, to the highly lucrative pharmaceutical companies. It was the development of an industrial method of producing ammonia early in the twentieth century which led to the production of artificial fertilizers. This process has revolutionized the growing of crops in recent times, alleviating food shortages in the developing world, and thus helping to eliminate poverty and disease, because a well-fed nation tends to be a healthy one. Many chemists work in forensic science, where their skills can be used in a wide range of identification processes, from drugs or alcohol in the blood, to recognition of specific fibres and dyes in clothing, to DNA testing, all of which help in many kinds of legal investigations.

Chemists, like all scientists, also have responsibilities. It seems unthinkable that a modern society will not continue to need more electricity. Coal stocks are huge, and can be used to fire power stations for the foreseeable future, but chemists are needed to find methods of preventing, or at least controlling, the accompanying emissions, such as carbon dioxide and sulfur dioxide, that contribute to global warming and acid rain, respectively, and poisonous emissions such as dioxins. Nuclear fuel gives us a cleaner process for generating electricity than burning coal, but can we find a way to dispose of the waste products safely? Modern society also faces increasing transport challenges, and it is the role of the chemist to create the catalysts that clean up the emissions from cars, preventing the noxious gases, such as carbon monoxide, and the oxides of nitrogen and sulfur, from entering the atmosphere, and to create the new batteries and fuel cells that will power the electric vehicles of the future. Pesticides and herbicides have led to increased yields of crops, benefiting countless people, but there have also been downsides to their use. DDT, for example, saved many lives, but had to be withdrawn when it was found to accumulate in body tissue and have a devastating effect on wildlife other than the targeted pests; but now malaria is again on the increase world-wide. Run-off from fields means that fertilizers and pesticides can get into the water supply, and it was an accident from a pesticide manufacturing plant in Bhopal, India in 1984, that released a chemical into the atmosphere that killed hundreds of people. Chemists have a duty of safety in their work, both in the ethics of what they are doing, and also in their working practices — to themselves and to the people around them. We shall try to explore all these roles.

In the next few pages we use nine short articles to show you the forefront of what is happening in the world of chemistry now. We don't expect you to understand all the science or all the terminology at the moment, but that is not important. What is vital is that you take from this introduction an impression of the vast range of work that is currently being carried out by chemists, and the importance of their work to our society. The chemistry that we teach later in the Course will enable you to understand and appreciate the science behind such advances.

In the final section we introduce you to the *Study File*. Among other things, this will give help in how to study, directions for using the Course Website, and instructions for the installation and use of all the software provided.

NEW FORMS OF CARBON

2

In 1996, Professor Harry Kroto, from the University of Sussex, and two American colleagues received the Nobel Prize for Chemistry. In 1985, they had discovered a completely new form of the element carbon. We are all familiar with some forms of carbon: it makes up the soft black amorphous particles in soot and charcoal, it occurs naturally in a soft crystalline form known as graphite, which we use for the 'lead' in pencils, and also, rarely, as the gemstone diamond, the hardest substance known. It is a truly versatile element.

Over the years, Harry Kroto's research had led him to look for molecules in the gas clouds of outer space, and he identified them by synthesising molecules in the laboratory and comparing their spectroscopic signals with the spectra collected by radiotelescopes. While trying to synthesise molecules with long linear carbon chains, he found unexpected lines in their mass spectra which he explained in terms of a previously unknown form of carbon; it consists of large spherical molecules, each with 60 carbon atoms joined together — just like a soccer ball — with rings of five carbon atoms connected to rings of six carbons (Figure 2.1). It was named buckminsterfullerene after the architect Buckminster Fuller, who designed geodesic domes with similar geometry.

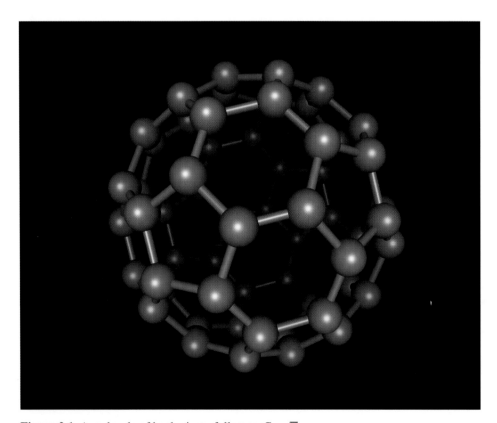

Figure 2.1 A molecule of buckminsterfullerene, C_{60}. 🖥

But what use are unusual looking molecules like this? Can this sort of research lead anywhere? Since 1985, Kroto's discovery has opened up a whole new field of research. Many more fullerene molecules have been synthesised, and they can now be made in many shapes and sizes (Figure 2.2), including sheets that roll up to form tubes — so-called 'nanotubes' (Figure 2.3). Nanotubes have been found to have the potential for storing large quantities of hydrogen, and may eventually be used as a safe way of transporting the hydrogen fuel needed for some electric cars.

Diamond is not only the hardest substance known, but is also the most effective conductor of heat known — better than silver or copper. Diamond films, therefore, could afford a superb, scratch-resistant surface or could be used to conduct heat away quickly — perhaps in sensitive miniature electrical circuits. Diamond films are difficult to grow, and up until now [2001] very high temperatures (800 °C or more) and high pressures have been used. Current research is investigating whether heating fullerene layers may provide a more economic, lower temperature route for doing this.

STUDY NOTE

The structures of graphite and diamond are discussed in Book 3 *The Third Dimension*, mass spectrometry in Book 8 *Separation, Purification and Identification*, and the chemistry of the fullerenes in Book 9 *Elements of the Earth*.

Figure 2.2
Sir Harry Kroto at the exhibition held to celebrate his discovery of buckminsterfullerene.

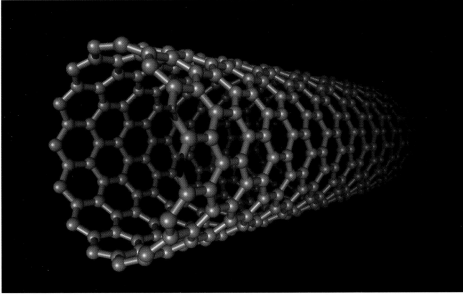

Figure 2.3 Computer model of a carbon nanotube. 💻

LIQUID CRYSTALS

3

Liquid crystals (Figure 3.1) are unusual in that they have some of the properties of a liquid and some of the properties of a crystalline solid; they are often known as the 'fourth state of matter'. They are viscous and can flow because the molecules are able to move about. But unlike a true liquid, where the molecules move at random, in a liquid crystal the molecules are partially aligned, tending to point in the same direction. Many liquid crystals are organic molecules and have a rod-like backbone containing benzene rings attached to long flexible carbon chains (Figure 3.2). Because these long, thin molecules are asymmetric, their properties are different in different directions: it is the uneven distribution of electric charge in a liquid crystal molecule, creating weak intermolecular forces, that causes the molecules to align along the direction of the chain.

Liquid crystals have properties that have been exploited to make a considerable impact on technology:

- the direction of alignment of the molecules can be reversed by a magnetic or an electric field;

- when polarized light passes through a liquid crystal, the plane of polarization of the light is rotated;

- the alignment of the molecules is temperature sensitive.

Figure 3.1
Liquid crystals.

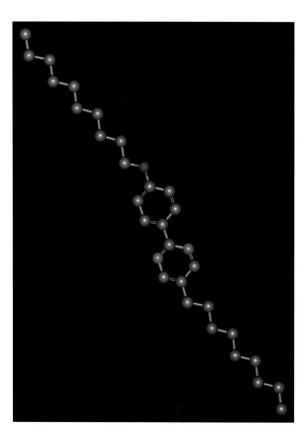

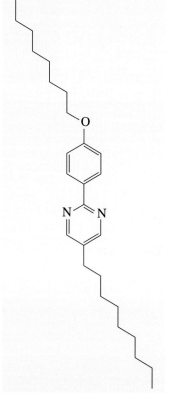

Figure 3.2
Typical liquid crystal molecule. 💻

These properties have been used to make the liquid crystal displays (LCDs) that we see so commonly in sensing devices (Figure 3.3), and in laptops, watches and calculators (Figure 3.4). Current research is directed at making larger, faster displays suitable for flat-screen computers and televisions (Figure 3.5b).

A high-resolution miniature liquid crystal display has been developed in Britain. It is known as SLIMDIS (silicon liquid crystal miniature display; Figure 3.6). It can be incorporated into a lightweight headset, where it provides visual information directly into the user's field of view, say surgeons or dentists, as they work. In the SLIMDIS device a liquid crystal layer has been mounted on a silicon backplane (which more than doubles the reflected light compared with traditional devices), incorporating 786 432 pixels of length 12 μm, thus giving a superb resolution of more than 25 000 lines per millimetre.

STUDY NOTE

Liquid crystals are discussed in the Case Study that accompanies Book 3 *The Third Dimension*.

Figure 3.3
LCD thermometer.

Figure 3.4
LCD display on a mobile phone.

(a)

(b)

Figure 3.6
The SLIMDIS display.

Figure 3.5 (a) Antiferroelectric liquid crystal, seen through a polarizing microscope, which may provide the faster 'switching times' vital for displays needed in, for example, (b) a flat computer screen.

ELECTRICAL BATTERIES

4

Imagine a car that you can start up and drive in almost total silence. Nor is this your only source of wellbeing! You can also bask in the knowledge that you are not polluting the air as you go. These are characteristics of an electric car, the transport of the future. But before the vision can be widely realized, chemists have work to do. Electric cars already exist (Figure 4.1), but they have serious drawbacks. The petrol engine is too formidable a competitor. For each kilo-gram of its mass, a tank of petrol can deliver about 10 000 watt-hours of energy. But the standard lead/acid car battery that starts your petrol engine and powers the milkman's cart produces no more than 50 watt-hours per kilo-gram. It is the mass of the metal electrodes and other components of the battery that is responsible for such low performance.

Figure 4.1
A modern electric car.

What is needed are new types of chemical reaction to generate electrical power inside a battery. The reactants must have a low density, and the reaction must deliver a lot of energy. For some time, long-term thinking has been focused on lithium. Lithium metal has a density so low that it floats on water. It also undergoes very energetic reactions, notably with oxygen, with which it forms solid lithium oxide, Li_2O, in which lithium ions, Li^+, are surrounded by oxide ions, O^{2-}.

Batteries containing free lithium metal, which reacts and ends up as lithium ions bound to oxide, are used in watches and pocket calculators. But to power cars, the batteries must be rechargeable, and suitable lithium metal is not easily regenerated in a recharging step.

One solution is the lithium ion battery, in which the lithium metal is combined with graphite in one of the electrodes (Figure 4.2). On discharge, the lithium moves out of the graphite as lithium ions, which pass through an electrolyte consisting of a lithium salt dissolved in either an organic solvent or polymer. They then enter the other electrode, which contains manganese dioxide, and become bound to oxygen. In charging mode, the lithium ions move back from the manganese dioxide to the graphite. This type of battery is already used to power laptop computers, but it still delivers less than 200 watt-hours per kilogram, and it has to be recharged at relatively short intervals. Much work remains to be done before such batteries become widely used for transport.

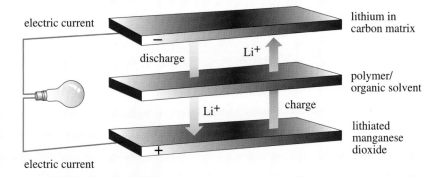

Figure 4.2 The principles of a so-called 'rocking-chair' lithium ion battery. The lithium ions 'rock' to and fro, moving from the graphite to the manganese dioxide host on discharge, and in the opposite direction during charging.

STUDY NOTE

Book 4 *Metals and Chemical Change* explains why lithium has the right properties for this sort of application, and the Case Study that accompanies Book 4 tells you more about advanced batteries and fuel cells.

CHEMISTRY AND DISEASE — PRACTICAL AND THEORETICAL APPROACHES

5

Proteins consist of long chains of amino acids — typically several hundred. The interatomic forces within and between these molecules cause the chains to fold into complex but highly organized three-dimensional shapes that govern their biological behaviour. If such proteins misfold, then the proteins can no longer carry out their biological role properly — as enzymes or receptors for instance — which can result in diseases such as cystic fibrosis. In one group of diseases the protein unfolds to form a pleated sheet-like form, known as a *fibril*, which can then aggregate and deposit in organs in the body (Figure 5.1). This effect is implicated in Parkinson's and Alzheimer's diseases, and in the prion protein diseases 'mad cow' disease, BSE, and its human form, variant CJD. Understanding how such proteins fold or misfold could provide important information for treating or preventing these diseases. One chemical approach has been to isolate the protein associated with a particular disease, and artificially make it unfold under laboratory conditions, using a denaturant such as urea, and then allow it to fold up again. This whole process can be followed by a spectroscopic technique known as NMR, which gives information on the bonding of the hydrogen atoms. Another approach uses computer modelling to investigate the bonding changes that are involved when a protein forms a fibril. Investigations have been made into a possible binding site in the PrP protein (Figure 5.2) of prions, which are the infectious agents causing BSE; it is thought that such a site may bind to a normal PrP protein, thus starting the aggregation process that forms the insoluble fibrils, which is then irreversible.

Computer modelling also makes a major input into the design of new drugs. The enzyme sialidase (Figure 5.3) is found on the outer coating of the flu virus, and is involved in the spread of the virus. The anti-flu drug Relenza™, which inhibits the operation of sialidase, was designed using computer modelling techniques.

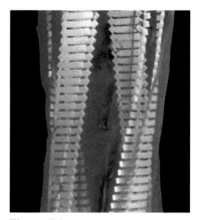

Figure 5.1
Amyloid fibrils.

STUDY NOTE

Molecular modelling is discussed in Book 6 *Molecular Modelling and Bonding*, and its application to drug design in the associated Case Study. NMR spectroscopy is discussed on the 'Spectroscopy' CD-ROM associated with Book 8 *Separation, Purification and Identification*.

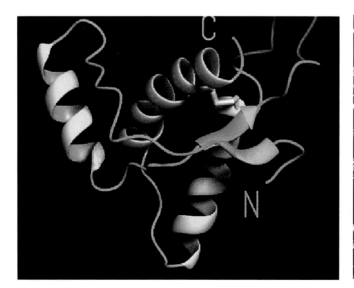

Figure 5.2 Domain containing amino acids 121–231 in the mouse PrP protein.

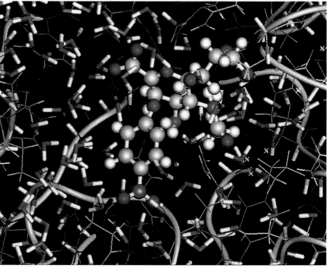

Figure 5.3 Computer-modelled structure of sialidase, an enzyme found in the outer coating of the flu virus.

FORENSIC SCIENCE

6

Forensic scientists have a huge range of problems to solve. They have to be able to distinguish if a particular poison or drug was responsible for a death, determine which explosive was used in a bomb, identify the dyes used in a particular piece of fabric, or trace a car through the paint used by the manufacturer. The identity of the person linked to a crime may be traced through evidence such as footprints, finger-prints, and, more recently, DNA analyses of body fluids and tissue. Chemical and spectroscopic methods of analysis lie at the heart of a forensic scientist's tools.

Fingerprints were traditionally highlighted by application of a very fine powder, which sticks to the greasy ridges of the prints, and then gently brushing away the excess powder before photographing the print. This process can easily damage a delicate print, and is not very effective on difficult surfaces such as wood, paper and plastic. A new powder has now been developed, which sticks to the fingerprint; it consists of fine flakes of iron with an organic coating. The powder is applied using an applicator incorporating strong magnets so that no brushes ever go near the print, hence reducing the risk of damage to the ridge pattern (Figure 6.1). Chemists have also found that spraying with ninhydrin (a blue-staining agent for amino acids) or exposure to the vapours from 'superglue' causes a fingerprint to develop a colour, which can be very useful in detecting fingerprints in inaccessible places!

STUDY NOTE

Forensic techniques are discussed in the Case Study that accompanies Book 8 *Separation, Purification and Identification*.

Figure 6.1
A new fingerprint powder has advantages over the old.

HIGH-TEMPERATURE SUPERCONDUCTORS

7

Superconductors are materials that, when cooled sufficiently, lose *all* their electrical resistance, and in addition expel all magnetic fields so that they are able to float over magnets (Figure 7.1). Clearly, such properties could have immense importance in the design of electronic devices, and in the transport of electricity.

Superconductivity was first discovered at the beginning of the twentieth century, and until recently the big snag was that it was a property only found in a few metals and alloys when they were cooled to extremely low temperatures using liquid helium. This meant that for many years superconductors were an interesting scientific phenomenon, but not of much practical use. However, two German chemists, Georg Bednorz and Alex Müller, discovered a mixed metal oxide of lanthanum, barium and copper which became superconducting at a significantly higher temperature. Research in this area then erupted, with many chemists all over the world involved in a race to find a room-temperature superconductor. The Holy Grail of a room-temperature superconductor has still not been found, but chemists have now managed to raise the superconducting transition temperature from 23 K (for a niobium/gallium alloy) to 135 K for a complex oxide containing mercury, thallium, calcium and copper.

Figure 7.2 depicts the crystal structure of $YBa_2Cu_3O_7$, the superconductor commonly known as YBCO, which was the first to be prepared that became superconducting above liquid nitrogen temperatures (77 K and below). Liquid nitrogen temperatures are much more easily accessible because liquid nitrogen is fairly cheap, and is easily transported and handled: you find it in every laboratory and hospital.

Crystallographers who have determined the structures of these fascinating compounds have found that they all have one feature in common, namely

Figure 7.1
A magnet floating over a superconductor.

that parallel planes of alternating copper and oxygen atoms spread throughout the structures.

The first devices using high-temperature superconductors have now been marketed. These are known as SQUIDS (superconducting quantum interference devices). They are able to detect minute changes in a magnetic field, and can be used by geologists to investigate such changes in the Earth's crust, and by medical researchers investigating diseases such as epilepsy (Figure 7.3).

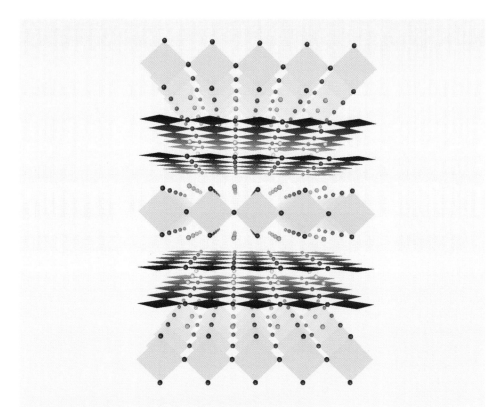

Figure 7.2
The crystal structure of the high-temperature superconductor $YBa_2Cu_3O_7$, commonly known as YBCO. The copper–oxygen planes are clearly visible in dark blue and the oxygen atoms are in red. 🖥

STUDY NOTE

Crystal structures and superconductivity are discussed in Book 3 *The Third Dimension*.

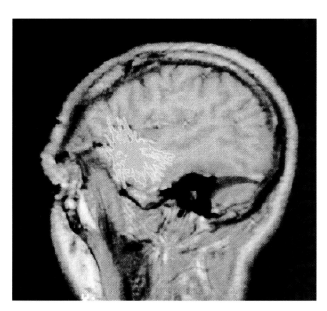

Figure 7.3 Focal epilepsy can arise from a localized neural defect that produces magnetic signals. An array of SQUIDs measures the signals, and the inferred position of the epileptic focus (yellow) is superimposed on a magnetic resonance image.

POLYMERS AND MATERIALS

8

Plastics are composed of very long chain molecules known as polymers, and their development has revolutionized modern life. Look around your house and you will find polythene (polyethene) bags, polyurethane foam cushions, polyester (PET, polyethene terephthalate) fabrics and fizzy drink bottles, nylon (polyamide) thread and clothes, PVC (polyvinyl chloride) window frames, polypropene car bumpers, Teflon-coated cooking pots, soft contact lenses, paints — and we could go on, the list is immense (Figure 8.1).

A polymer is made up of repeating identical small molecules known as 'monomers', which link together during a chemical process to form a very long chain with a high molecular mass (Figure 8.2). The chains are flexible, giving many plastics a 'rubbery' feel. When chemical bonds are formed *between* the long polymers (so-called 'cross-linking'), the polymers become less flexible but are mechanically stronger.

(a)

(b)

(c)

(d)

Figure 8.1 Different uses for polymers.

STUDY NOTE
Polymer formation is discussed in Book 10 *Mechanism and Synthesis,* and the Case Study
that accompanies it looks at the polymers used for soft contact lenses.

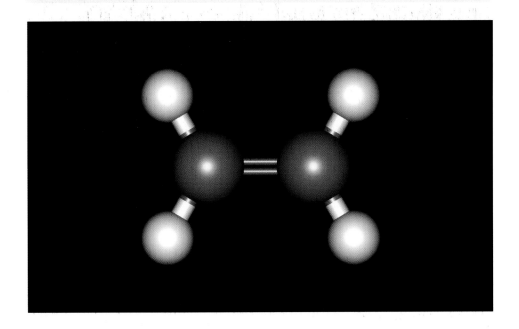

Figure 8.2
The polythene (polyethene) polymer,
and its monomer ethene.

CHEMISTRY AND DISEASE — SYNTHETIC APPROACHES

9

Some synthetic organic chemists have turned to sea-creatures for inspiration in drug synthesis. Sea-creatures do not appear to suffer from illnesses in the same way that we do. Simple creatures such as barnacles and sponges do not make antibodies to fight off infection, but rather manufacture complex chemicals which fight off the bacteria and viruses, and kill off any mutant cancer cells. These chemicals can now be isolated and investigated for their activity against various diseases in humans. If a compound is found to be biologically active, chemists first set about determining the structure of the molecule, and then try to synthesise it (or something similar) in the laboratory.

Barnacles (Figure 9.1) are found to contain a compound known as bryostatin 1 (Figure 9.2), which is a potent anticancer agent for some ovarian and skin cancers. However, it takes one tonne of barnacles to produce 500 mg of bryostatin 1! So this is where the synthetic chemist comes in, working out a route to make the molecule. The chemists work backwards: a complex molecule such as bryostatin 1 is conceptually broken down into much smaller chunks which could be synthesised more easily, and then a route for joining the parts together is sought. For complex molecules, this so-called 'retrosynthetic analysis' may take many steps, and years of work.

Another source of possible new drugs is based on compounds called mycalamides, which have been isolated from the Mycale sponge found in Otago Harbour, New Zealand (Figure 9.3) and have been found to be very active against viruses and cancer. These compounds (Figure 9.4) also act as powerful immunosupressants, so they could be important in transplant surgery. As well as investigating other marine sponges, chemists are also examining the activity of chemicals released by the sea slug. With the rich diversity of life in the oceans, there should be plenty of material for chemists to look at for many years to come!

Figure 9.1
Barnacles.

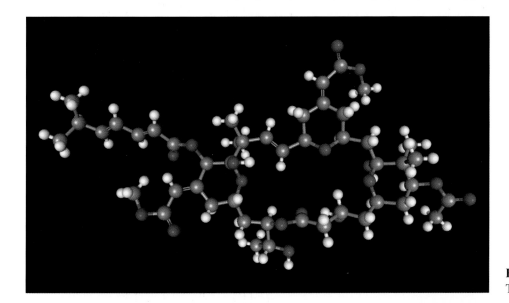

Figure 9.2
The bryostatin 1 molecule. 🖳

Figure 9.3
The Mycale sponge found in Otago
Harbour.

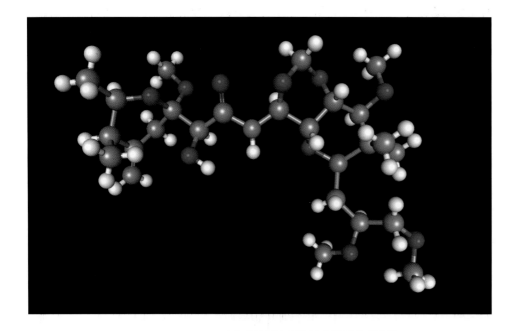

Figure 9.4
A new derivative of mycalamide — 18-*O*-methylmycalamide B.

STUDY NOTE

Isolating and characterizing new compounds is discussed in Book 8 *Isolation, Purification and Identification*. Retrosynthetic analysis is discussed in Book 10 *Mechanism and Synthesis*.

BALL LIGHTNING

Besides helping us to make new products, cure disease and solve crimes, chemistry also takes centre stage when we try to understand how the world works. For example, widely accepted explanations of global warming rest on the properties of molecules. A more mysterious natural phenomenon that needs an explanation of this sort is ball lightning.

Everyone is familiar with the common type of lightning, shown in Figure 10.1 as a jagged discharge or 'bolt'. Ball lightning is very different. It consists of a glowing sphere of light, about the size of a grapefruit, which usually appears out of thin air during thundery weather. The spheres float close to the ground, drifting slowly for about 20 seconds before expiring. There have been recorded sightings of ball lightning going back to the Middle Ages, but very few people ever see it. A few

Figure 10.1
The familiar but spectacular lightning bolt.

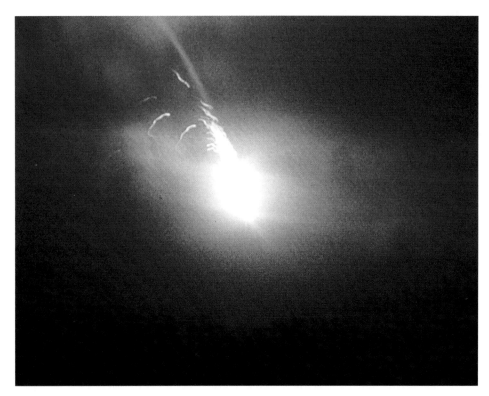

Figure 10.2
A photograph of ball lightning taken in Austria in 1978. It has a white centre that extends into a luminous tail, and there is a blue surround. This makes it even more striking than the ordinary spherical sort, which prompted the explanation given in the text.

photographs exist (Figure 10.2), but as yet, there are no known videotapes. Until recently, there was no convincing scientific explanation for the phenomenon; it sounds, in fact, like something from the realm of UFOs.

In 2000, two chemical engineers in New Zealand, John Abrahamson and James Dinniss, produced a new and promising explanation. It runs as follows. A conventional lightning strike on soil can generate temperatures as high as 3 000 K. At such temperatures, silicates or silica could then react with carbon from the organic matter in the soil to produce a vapour containing silicon atoms. This vapour is blown into the air by the shock wave of the lightning strike. As the silicon atoms cool, they combine to form a buoyant fluff ball composed of chains of tiny particles of solid silicon. This fluff ball burns steadily in air as the finely divided silicon combines with oxygen to regenerate SiO_2. When the silicon has been consumed, the glowing sphere disappears.

Abrahamson and Dinniss exposed soil to a lightning-like discharge in the laboratory. Although they did not observe ball lightning, they did find the required chains of tiny silicon particles in the air space close to the strike. This is promising. Experiments are under way to find the soil and discharge conditions that might generate ball lightning.

STUDY NOTE

The energies of the kinds of chemical reaction that are believed to produce ball lightning are discussed in Book 4 *Metals and Chemical Change*.

WHAT NEXT?

The last nine sections have been designed to whet your appetite for the huge variety of chemistry that is to follow. But now to work! Book 2, which follows, revises and broadens your understanding of the chemical concepts you have studied previously.

To begin with, you should familiarize yourself with some of the tools that we are providing *before* moving on to Book 2.

First of all, find and open your *Study File*. If you have not already done so, clip into it all the documents listed on the *Study File* contents page. (Don't worry if everything isn't there; some items will arrive in a later mailing.)

11.1 The *Study File*

The *Study File* contains a variety of different resources. Among other things, you will find advice on developing *transferable skills*, material on the use of *library resources*, instructions for the installation and use of all the *software* associated with the Course, an introduction to using the *internet* and to our *website*, and a section on the naming of chemical compounds.

You can also use the *Study File* to store booklets such as the S205 *Course Guide*, the S205 *Glossary* and the S205 *Data Book* if you wish.

Use the rest of your study time for Book 1 to familiarize yourself with each of these resources.

11.1.1   Introducing transferable skills

You will find the information and advice on developing skills and good study techniques in 'Introducing transferable skills' in the *Study File*.

SKILLS ACTIVITY

You should spend about an hour on 'Introducing transferable skills' and its associated activities.

11.1.2   Finding and accessing information

You will find the material on searching for information and using the library in 'Introducing transferable skills' in the *Study File*.

FINDING INFORMATION ACTIVITY

You should spend about 3 hours on 'Finding and accessing information' and its associated activities.

11.1.3   WebLab ViewerLite

WebLab ViewerLite is a software package that enables us to view and rotate 3-D models of molecules and crystal structures. The software is on the CD-ROM that accompanies this Book. The instructions for installing it can be found in the 'Computer Guide' (in the *Study File*). More extensive help files are included in the program itself. Many of the molecules and structures throughout the Course will be available to view using this medium, and all such structures will be indicated by the symbol 🖥. In Book 1 the molecules in Figures 1.1, 1.2, 1.3, 1.5, 2.1, 2.3, 3.2, 7.2, 8.2, 9.2 and 9.4 can all be viewed using WebLab ViewerLite.

WEBLAB VIEWERLITE ACTIVITY

You should install the WebLab ViewerLite software on your computer now, and use it to look at the molecules for Book 1, which can be found in the 'Figures' folder .

This exercise will take you about 1 hour.

11.1.4   The S205 website

You will find instructions in the 'Computer Guide' of the *Study File* for gaining access to the S205 website. The website provides up-to-date information on the Course, some course material such as the *Study Calendar*, access to a FirstClass conference, and to some useful websites.

USING THE S205 WEBSITE

The different features of the website are explained in detail in the 'Computer Guide' of the *Study File*, and you should take some time now to familiarize yourself with how to use them.

11.1.5   StarOffice

StarOffice is a fully featured 'Office' package, offering word processing, spread-sheet, presentation, drawing and other functions. If you already have an 'Office' type package such as Microsoft Office, we would recommend that you carry on using what you know. However, if you do not have an 'Office' system, StarOffice has a lot to offer, and we show some of the things that you can do with it in the 'Computer Guide' of the *Study File*.

Acknowledgements

Grateful acknowledgement is made to the following sources for permission to reproduce material in this book:

Cover

Copyright © 1996 PhotoDisc, Inc.

Figures

Figures 1.4, 2.2, 3.1, 3.5a, 3.6, 5.1, 5.3, 6.1, 9.1 and 9.3: Courtesy of the Engineering and Physical Sciences Research Council; *Figure 3.4*: Courtesy of Sharn Inc.; Figure 3.5b: Copyright © 1996 PhotoDisc, Inc.; *Figure 4.1*: Courtesy of Ballard Power Systems: *Figure 5.2*: Reprinted by permission from Nature www.nature.com 382. Copyright 1996 Macmillan Magazines Limited; *Figure 7.1*: Texas Center for Superconductivity at the University of Houston; *Figure 7.3*: Scripps Research Institute; *Figures 8.1a and 10.1*: A P Photos; *Figure 8.1b*: Plysu; *Figure 8.1c*: Cantor & Nissel; *Figure 8.1d*: Ford Motor Company Limited; Figure 10.2: Fortean Picture Library.

Every effort has been made to trace all the copyright owners, but if any has been inadvertently overlooked, the publishers will be pleased to make the necessary arrangements at the first opportunity.

BOOK 2
INTRODUCING THE MOLECULAR WORLD

CONTENTS

INTRODUCTION

Book 1 supplied you with a brief outline of just some of the important problems and topics that are being studied by the chemists of today. S205 *The Molecular World* will provide you with a detailed understanding of these topics, and of the ways in which the associated problems might be solved by chemical methods. But to acquire this understanding you must have a good grasp of fundamental chemical ideas. Here, in Book 2 *Introducing the Molecular World*, you will start to get it. Book 2 has two main purposes. Firstly, it will revise, and in some cases extend, some important concepts with which you should already be partly familiar. You will then be better equipped to understand the detail of the Books that are to come.

Secondly, the revision process will allow us to explain how the different parts of the Course fit together to form a coherent whole. This task is performed under seven main headings and an overview. Each of those headings consists of a general idea of great importance to chemists. We begin with the idea that comes closest to defining the nature of chemistry itself.

EVERYTHING THAT YOU CAN SEE IS MADE OF ATOMS

The idea that everything that we can see is an assembly of tiny particles called atoms is chemistry's greatest contribution to science. There are about 120 known kinds of atom, and each one is distinguished by a name, by a chemical symbol, and by a number called the **atomic number**. The meaning of atomic number is best understood from the Rutherford model of the atom (Figure 2.1). Each atom has a tiny positively charged *nucleus*, where nearly all of its mass resides. Around this nucleus move negatively charged particles called *electrons*. Any atom is electrically neutral, but each electron carries a negative charge, to which we give the symbol $-e$.

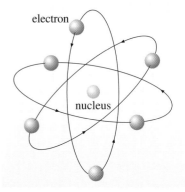

Figure 2.1
The Rutherford model of the atom.

⬤ So what is the charge carried by the nucleus of the atom in Figure 2.1?

⬤ $+6e$; the atom in Figure 2.1 contains six electrons whose total charge will be $-6e$. To generate an overall charge of zero, the positive charge on the nucleus must be $+6e$.

In fact, the positive charge on the nucleus of any atom is provided by minute positively charged particles called *protons*, each of which carries a charge of $+e$.

⬤ How many protons are there in the nucleus of the atom in Figure 2.1?

⬤ 6; the nucleus carries a total charge of $+6e$, and each proton has a charge of $+e$.

The atomic number of an atom is the number of protons in its nucleus. It is also equal to the number of electrons in the neutral atom. The atomic number of the atom in Figure 2.1 is therefore six.

2.1 Chemical elements

Atoms of the same atomic number behave virtually identically in chemical reactions. They are therefore given the same chemical name and chemical symbol. For example, the atom of atomic number 6, which is shown in Figure 2.1, is a carbon atom, whose symbol is C. All materials are made of atoms, but there is a special class of substance whose members consist of atoms of the same atomic number. They are called **chemical elements** and about 120 of them are known. Each element is allocated a name and a chemical symbol which is the same as that given to the atoms it contains. Thus, the element carbon (C), which is the major constituent of pencil 'leads', consists entirely of carbon atoms (C), all with atomic number 6. Six other examples are shown in Figure 2.2. Before the nineteenth century, such substances were recognized as materials that defied all attempts to break them down into simpler chemical components. Chemistry's greatest contributions to scientific thought can all be traced back to the subsequent marriage of this concept of a chemical element with the atomic theory (see Box 2.1).

One of the implications of this Section, and of Figure 2.2, is that chemical symbols have two meanings: they can represent either a chemical element or a type of atom. Thus, the symbol S can represent either the yellow solid in Figure 2.2c, or the type of atom of which that solid is composed. With experience, you will find that when you meet chemical symbols, the context will reveal which meaning is appropriate.

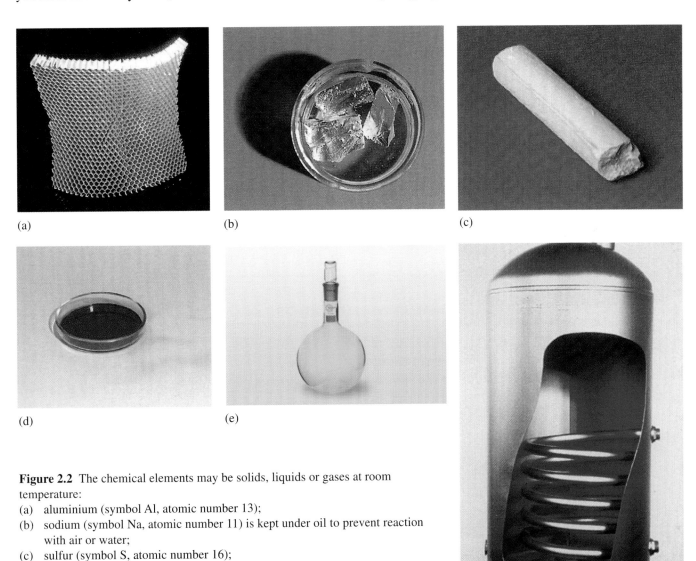

(a)   (b)   (c)

(d)   (e)

Figure 2.2 The chemical elements may be solids, liquids or gases at room temperature:
(a) aluminium (symbol Al, atomic number 13);
(b) sodium (symbol Na, atomic number 11) is kept under oil to prevent reaction with air or water;
(c) sulfur (symbol S, atomic number 16);
(d) bromine (symbol Br, atomic number 35) is a dark-red liquid;
(e) chlorine (symbol Cl, atomic number 17) is a yellow–green gas;
(f) copper (symbol Cu, atomic number 29).

(f)

BOX 2.1 Atoms in view?

The Greek philosophers Democritus (460–370BC) and Epicurus (340–270BC) believed in a world made of tiny hard atoms in endless motion. Their ideas have come down to us through a poem, De Rerum Natura ('The Way Things Are'), written by the Roman poet Lucretius (90–40BC). Lucretius was profoundly hostile to contemporary ideas of an after-life, in which there was punishment by the gods for former sins. This turned the atomic theory into useful propaganda. After death, one's atoms were dispersed into the larger world and assumed new forms. So there could be no question of reassembly for punishment:

> …all our atoms went
> Wandering here and there and far away
> So we must think of death as being nothing,
> As less than sleep, or less than nothing even,
> Since our array of matter never stirs
> To reassemble, once the chill of death
> Has taken over.

> *Lucretius*

Atoms became a part of modern science when John Dalton (1766–1844) suggested that the atoms of each element are identical, especially in mass. Ultimately, this was proved wrong because of the discovery of isotopes (Section 2.1.1), but it was also immensely fruitful. Even in 1900, there were eminent scientists who did not believe in the reality of atoms. But between 1900 and 1920, phenomena as varied as the motion of pollen grains in water, diffusion in liquids, radioactivity and the diffraction of X-rays by crystals, all gave similar values for the *sizes* of atoms. This convergence of data from such different directions destroyed any serious opposition.

In scanning tunnelling microscopy (STM), a small voltage is applied between a 'probe' and a surface that the probe moves across. The observed current is sensitive to the surface contours at an atomic level, and its variation can be stored, computer enhanced and plotted out as a map of the surface (Figure 2.3). This technique earned Gerd Binning and Heinrich Rohrer of IBM's Zurich Laboratory the 1986 Nobel Prize for Physics. It is the nearest one can get to 'seeing atoms'. But how do we know that it is atoms that are displayed on the computer screen rather than, say, some microscopic set of dentures? The answer is that their size agrees with the values obtained by the classical methods mentioned above. Both classical and modern methods give similar values for atomic size. Pictures like Figure 2.3 have only enhanced a convergence that already existed in the results of other methods.

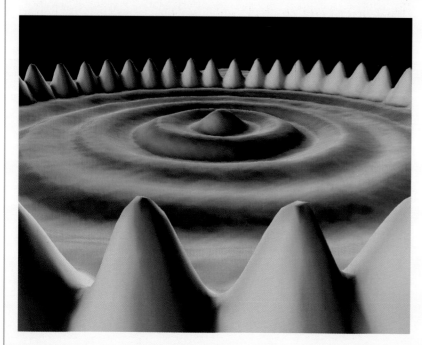

Figure 2.3 A ring of 48 iron atoms on a copper surface observed by STM. Notice the wave-like crests and troughs inside the ring. These are thought to be due to the wave-like properties of electrons confined within the ring.

2.1.1 Isotopes

All atoms of the same element have identical atomic numbers, and are chemically similar, but they may not be identical in other ways. Figure 2.2f shows copper. All copper atoms have atomic number 29: all their nuclei contain 29 protons. But they also contain *uncharged* particles called *neutrons*. In natural copper, the atoms are of two kinds. One has 29 protons and 34 neutrons in the nucleus; the other has 29 protons and 36 neutrons (Figure 2.4).

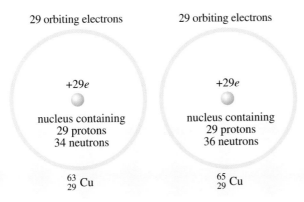

Figure 2.4 The distribution of protons, neutrons and electrons in the atoms of the two isotopes of copper present in copper metal. In both cases, the atomic number is 29: there are 29 protons in the nucleus. This makes both types of atom, atoms of copper, but they differ in the number of neutrons contained in their nucleus.

The two different kinds of atom are called *isotopes* of copper. The neutron has a mass very similar to that of the proton, so the two isotopes differ in mass. The sum of the numbers of neutrons and protons for a particular isotope is called the *mass number*.

⬤ What are the mass numbers of the two copper isotopes in Figure 2.4?

⬤ 63 and 65 — that is, (29 + 34) and (29 + 36), respectively.

The two isotopes are written $^{63}_{29}$Cu and $^{65}_{29}$Cu, where the mass number and atomic number precede the chemical symbol as a superscript and subscript, respectively (Figure 2.5).

The mass number of any isotope is equal to the relative atomic mass of its atom, rounded to the nearest whole number. The atoms of natural copper are about 70% $^{63}_{29}$Cu and 30% $^{65}_{29}$Cu. Thus, the relative atomic mass of natural copper (63.5) lies between 63 and 65, but closer to 63 because that is the relative atomic mass of the more abundant isotope. But although copper contains two different isotopes, each isotope has the same atomic number, and therefore a virtually identical chemistry.

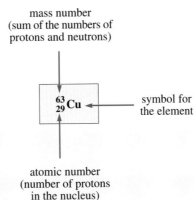

Figure 2.5
A symbolism showing the number of neutrons, protons and electrons in the neutral atom of an isotope.

2.2 Chemical compounds

Chemical elements contain atoms of the same atomic number. But most materials consist of *chemical compounds*. These are a combination of the atoms of two or more chemical elements. Such combinations often occur in simple numerical ratios. Thus, when sodium metal (Figure 2.2b) and chlorine gas (Figure 2.2e) are brought into contact, they react vigorously, and white crystals of common salt (sodium chloride) are formed. In these crystals, there are equal numbers of sodium and chlorine atoms; that is, the sodium and chlorine atoms are combined in the simple ratio 1 : 1. This is expressed by writing sodium chloride as NaCl. In this formula, there is one chlorine atom (Cl) for every sodium atom (Na).

Likewise, aluminium (Figure 2.2a) and liquid bromine (Figure 2.2d) will react violently after a short interval, and yield a white solid called aluminium bromide. In this solid there are three bromine atoms for every aluminium atom.

⬤ Write a chemical formula for aluminium bromide.

⬤ $AlBr_3$; the subscript three following the bromine marks the fact that the Al : Br atomic ratio is 1 : 3.

Formulae such as NaCl and $AlBr_3$ tell us the ratios in which atoms are combined in compounds. When they are written down, the ratio is reduced to the lowest possible whole number, and the chemical formulae obtained in this way are then called **empirical formulae**. Most chemical elements are metals, and the formulae quoted for compounds of these metallic elements are usually empirical formulae. But they tell us nothing about the way that the atoms are grouped within the compound. For this, we need formulae of a different type.

2.3 Molecular substances

Chlorine, bromine and iodine belong to a family of elements called the *halogens*. At room temperature, chlorine (Figure 2.2e) is a gas, bromine (Figure 2.2d) is a liquid and iodine is a dark-purple solid. All three substances are chemical elements. One's first thought might be that the tiny particles of which, say, chlorine gas is composed are single atoms.

⬤ Is this the case?

⬤ No; the tiny particles or *molecules* consist of pairs of chlorine atoms, Cl_2.

A gas, like chlorine, occupies much more space than a solid or liquid, so the distance between the molecules is comparatively large. At normal temperatures and pressures, it averages about 3 500 pm (1 pm $\equiv 10^{-12}$ m), compared with a distance of only 198 pm separating the chlorine atoms in gaseous Cl_2 molecules (Figure 2.6a). This disparity is less extreme, but still evident in liquid bromine and solid iodine. The positions of atoms in solids can be determined by X-ray crystallography. In solid iodine (Figure 2.6b), each iodine atom has a second iodine atom at a distance of only 271 pm. By contrast, in other directions, the shortest distance to another iodine atom is considerably greater (350 pm). So the iodine atoms can be grouped into pairs; hence we conclude that solid iodine contains I_2 molecules.

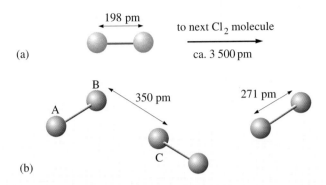

Figure 2.6 (a) The distance between the atoms in Cl_2 molecules is small compared with the average distance between the molecules in a jar of chlorine gas. On the scale set by our Cl_2 molecule, that average distance puts the next Cl_2 molecule on the opposite page. (b) In solid iodine, I_2 molecules (e.g. AB) can be identified through their separation by a distance of 271 pm. These molecules are separated by longer distances of at least 350 pm (BC).

Similar reasoning can be used to identify molecules in compounds. At room temperature, carbon dioxide is a gas containing CO_2 molecules. On cooling, it becomes a solid ('dry ice'). In dry ice (Figure 2.7), each carbon atom, A, has two oxygen atom neighbours, B and C, at a distance of 116 pm. These three atoms are colinear. The next nearest atom is another oxygen, D, at 311 pm. Here is evidence that solid carbon dioxide contains linear CO_2 molecules, with the atom sequence O—C—O.

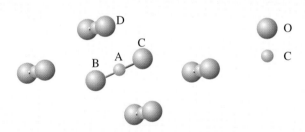

Figure 2.7 The environment of a carbon atom, labelled A, in solid carbon dioxide, 'dry ice'. Note that molecule BAC is in the plane of the paper; the other four molecules shown are not.

The formulae Cl_2, Br_2, I_2 and CO_2 that we have identified for the three halogens and carbon dioxide are called **molecular formulae**. They tell us how the atoms are grouped together in the molecules from which the substance is built up. Likewise, the four substances are called *molecular substances* because they have structures that allow discrete molecules to be picked out. So far, we have examined just one molecular compound (CO_2) and its molecular formula is identical with its empirical formula, but often this is not so. In Section 2.2, we discussed solid aluminium bromide with empirical formula $AlBr_3$. Here, the molecular and empirical formulae are not identical: the crystal structure contains Al_2Br_6 molecules (Figure 2.8).

○ Do these molecules have the same empirical formula as the solid in which they are found?

○ Yes; the molecular formula is Al_2Br_6, but in both the molecules and the solid, the ratio of aluminium atoms to bromine atoms is $1 : 3$. In molecular substances that contain just one type of molecule, that molecule has the same empirical formula as the compound.

One particular group of molecular substances is so important that three of the ten Books of S205 are largely given over to it. The organic compounds that are studied in Books 5, 7 and 10 are almost entirely molecular. To mark this point, we show, in Figure 2.9, the grouping of the atoms in the molecules of two important solid organic compounds. Figure 2.9a shows the structure of aspirin, the best-known pain-killer, which is also used in the precautionary treatment of heart conditions. The molecule in Figure 2.9b is RDX, the most common military high explosive. Here, you need not worry about the names used for organic compounds. In this Book, relatively few such compounds are discussed, and we shall be concerned only with differences in the *structure* of their molecules; the names are just labels. Later, in Book 3, you will receive a proper introduction to organic nomenclature, and the meaning behind the names will become clearer.

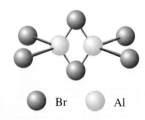

Br   Al

Figure 2.8
The structure of the Al_2Br_6 molecule. The two aluminium atoms, and four of the bromine atoms at the ends of the molecule, lie in the same plane (at right-angles to the plane of the paper). The two bromines that bridge the aluminiums lie above and below this plane.

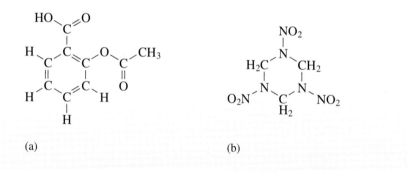

(a)   (b)

Figure 2.9 Molecules of: (a) acetylsalicylic acid (aspirin); (b) 1,3,5-trinitroperhydro-1,3,5-triazine, also known as RDX (Research Department Explosive!) or cyclonite.

2.4 Non-molecular substances

Non-molecular substances defy attempts to pick out discrete molecules from their structures. One example is common salt, NaCl, which is built up from the tiny cubes shown in Figure 2.10a. Look first at the sodium at the centre of the cube.

○ What kind of atom is closest to the sodium, and how many of them are there?

○ The sodium is surrounded by six chlorines at the centres of the cube faces.

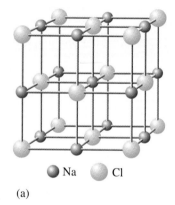

Na   Cl

(a)

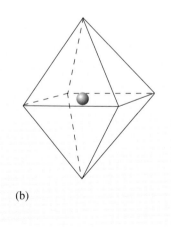

(b)

Figure 2.10
(a) Structure of common salt or sodium chloride; (b) a regular octahedron whose corners represent the positions of the chlorines around each sodium.

42

The six chlorines lie at the corners of a three-dimensional figure called a regular octahedron (a solid figure with eight faces; see Figure 2.10b). The formula NaCl for sodium chloride is an empirical formula: it merely tells us that in sodium chloride there are equal numbers of sodiums and chlorines. This condition is automatically fulfilled when many cubes of the Figure 2.10a type are joined through their faces. But Figure 2.10 provides no evidence that NaCl is the *molecular formula* of sodium chloride. Indeed, quite the opposite, because the six chlorines around the sodium in Figure 2.10a all lie the *same distance* away. There are no grounds for singling out just one of them and coupling it with the sodium as an NaCl molecule. There is no evidence of discrete NaCl molecules in the solid; NaCl is a *non-molecular* compound, and the concept of a 'molecular formula' is not appropriate in solid NaCl.

Similar considerations apply to silicon dioxide or silica, SiO_2. This is the main component of sand, and it has the same type of empirical formula as carbon dioxide. In solid carbon dioxide, two of the oxygen atoms around each carbon were much closer than the others, so we could identify a CO_2 molecule. However, in silica (Figure 2.11), each silicon atom sits at the centre of a tetrahedron of oxygen atoms: the silicon is surrounded by four oxygen atoms, all at the same distance of 162 pm. There is no evidence of discrete SiO_2 molecules.

Most of the chemical elements are non-molecular substances. Figure 2.12 shows the environment of each atom in diamond and metallic aluminium. In diamond (Figure 2.12a), there are four surrounding carbon atoms at the corners of a regular tetrahedron, and the C—C distance is 154 pm. In aluminium (Figure 2.12b), there are twelve surrounding aluminium atoms, and the Al—Al distance is 286 pm. There is no justification for dividing the structure up into molecules containing two or more atoms. Any such 'molecule' extends throughout a crystal of the substance, and its formula will vary with the crystal size. For this reason, the phrase **extended structure** is sometimes used to describe non-molecular substances.

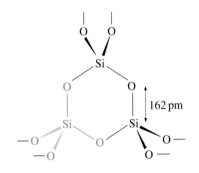

Figure 2.11
The structure of silica, SiO_2, in the form of quartz. One SiO_4 tetrahedron is highlighted in green.

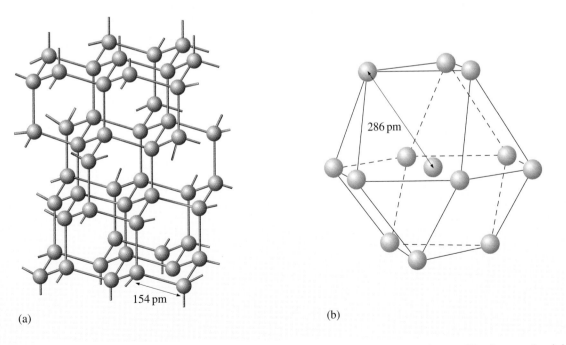

(a)

(b)

Figure 2.12 The environment of each atom in (a) the diamond form of the element carbon; (b) the metallic element aluminium. Both substances are non-molecular, and have extended structures.

In Figures 2.12a and 2.12b, the extension occurs in three dimensions, but it may sometimes reveal itself in only one or two. Figure 2.13 shows the structure of graphite, the form of carbon used in pencil 'leads'. There are regular hexagons of carbon atoms arranged in parallel sheets. Within the sheets, the C—C distance is only 142 pm, but the shortest distances between the sheets is 340 pm.

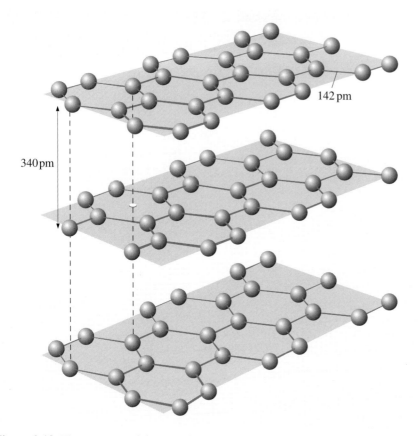

142 pm

340 pm

Figure 2.13 The structure of the graphite form of the element carbon.

If one regards a single crystal of graphite as an extended structure, does the extension occur in one, two or three dimensions?

In two; the internuclear distances allow us to break the structure up into two-dimensional sheets extending throughout the entire crystal.

These sheets, however, are not repeating molecules because, again, their size varies with the size of the crystal. Graphite is therefore classified as a non-molecular substance with an extended structure.

Figures 2.12a and 2.13 show that the element carbon occurs in different solid forms, each of which has a different structure. These different solid forms of the same element are known as **allotropes** (or *polymorphs*). Phosphorus, sulfur and tin are other examples of elements that occur as more than one allotrope.

2.5 Binding forces in molecular and non-molecular substances — a first look

As we shall see in Section 5, elementary bonding theories imply that materials as different as salt, iodine and aluminium are held together by different types of chemical bond. However, all binding forces between atoms are essentially electrical, and arise from a balance of forces acting between positively charged nuclei and negatively charged electrons. As electrical forces are stronger at short distances, in solid iodine (Figure 2.6b) the short distances between the pairs of atoms (I_2 molecules) suggest that the forces holding these atoms together are strong. By contrast, the longer distance between different pairs (molecules) tells us that the forces acting between one I_2 molecule and another are much weaker.

Now, iodine melts at only 114 °C and boils at 185 °C.

● Why does iodine have low melting and boiling temperatures?

● In solid iodine, different I_2 molecules are held together by weak forces, so only a little thermal energy is needed to separate them and create first a liquid, and then a gas. Both liquid and gaseous iodine also contain I_2 molecules. To melt and then boil iodine it is not necessary to break up the I_2 molecules themselves.

This also explains another property of iodine: it dissolves fairly easily in an organic solvent like petrol. The solid crystal falls apart and individual I_2 molecules drift off into solution. As organic compounds are molecular, they too, often dissolve in petrol. The organic polymers you meet in everyday life have unusually large molecules, but being molecular they may also be vulnerable (Figure 2.14).

Fuel hoarder sentenced

BY MAURICE WEAVER

A TAXI driver who tried to beat the fuel crisis by storing petrol in a wheelie-bin at home was given a suspended prison sentence yesterday.

Saquib Bashir, 28, caused a major alert, leading to the evacuation of 60 neighbouring properties and a £100,000 clean-up bill when fuel melted the bottom of the plastic bin and leaked into the cellar of his terraced house.

At Derby Crown Court,

Bashir admitted storing petrol without a licence and in non-metal containers.

He was sentenced to eight months' imprisonment, suspended for two years, and ordered to pay £1,000 costs.

Bashir had stockpiled 90 litres of fuel in a wheelie-bin, a beer barrel and a cooking-oil container at his home in Normanton, Derby.

Later he told trading standards officers that he had no idea that petrol was so flammable.

Figure 2.14
From the *Daily Telegraph*, 6 April 2001. (Note the erroneous use of 'melt' for 'dissolve' in this extract.)

By contrast, in salt, silica or aluminium, the bonding is more evenly distributed through the crystal, and there are no points of weakness where discrete molecules can be prised apart. So the melting and boiling temperatures of non-molecular substances tend to be greater than those of molecular ones. Salt, silica and aluminium, for example, melt at 801 °C, 1 713 °C and 660 °C, respectively.

2.6 Summary of Section 2

1   All materials are made of atoms of about 120 different chemical elements, each element being characterized by an atomic number which lies in the range 1–120.

2   Each atom has a nucleus where most of its mass resides. The atomic number is equal to the number of units of positive charge on the nucleus, the number of protons in the nucleus, and to the number of surrounding electrons in the neutral atom.

3   The nuclei of nearly all atoms contain neutrons as well as protons. The mass number of an atom is the sum of the numbers of neutrons and protons.

4   All atoms of an element contain the same number of protons, but they may differ in the number of neutrons. This gives rise to atoms of an element with the same atomic number but different mass numbers. These different types of atom are called isotopes. In chemical changes isotopes behave almost identically.

5   Chemical compounds are combinations of the atoms of two or more chemical elements. The empirical formula of a compound tells us the ratio in which the atoms of its elements are combined.

6   Molecular substances have structures from which discrete molecules can be picked out by using interatomic distance as a criterion; non-molecular substances do not. The formula of these discrete molecules is called the molecular formula. Most molecular compounds contain just one type of molecule, which then has the same empirical formula as the compound. Most organic compounds are molecular substances.

7   Molecular substances usually have lower melting and boiling temperatures than non-molecular ones. They also tend to dissolve more easily in organic solvents such as petrol.

QUESTION 2.1

The element aluminium (symbol Al; atomic number 13) has a relative atomic mass of 27.0; in nature it contains just one isotope.

(a) State the number of protons in the aluminium nucleus.

(b) State the number of orbiting electrons around the nucleus of an aluminium atom.

(c) If the electronic charge is written $-e$, what is the total charge on the nucleus of the aluminium atom?

(d) State the number of neutrons in the aluminium nucleus.

(e) Write down the isotope that is present in natural aluminium by combining mass number, atomic number and chemical symbol.

QUESTION 2.2

The molecular formula of an oxide of phosphorus is P_4O_{10}.

(a) What is the empirical formula of the oxide?

(b) Can the empirical formula of a molecular compound consisting of one type of molecule, contain more atoms than its molecular formula? Explain your answer.

QUESTION 2.3

Figure 2.15a shows the structure of solid hydrogen fluoride, HF, which consists of zigzag chains containing hydrogen and fluorine atoms. Figure 2.15b shows the structure of solid silicon carbide, SiC.

(a) Classify the compounds as molecular or non-molecular.

(b) One of the compounds (X) melts at $-83\,°C$ and is slightly soluble in petrol. The other (Y) remains solid even at $2\,500\,°C$ and is insoluble in petrol. Which is which? Explain your answer.

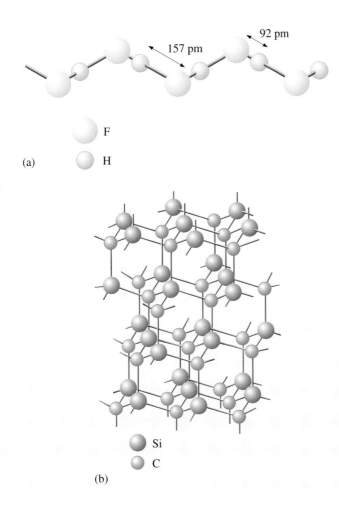

(a)

F

H

(b)

Si

C

Figure 2.15 The structures of: (a) zigzag chains in solid hydrogen fluoride; (b) solid silicon carbide, in which all distances between atoms linked by lines are 165 pm.

CHEMICAL PATTERNS ARE TO BE FOUND IN THE PERIODIC TABLE

3

The chemistry of the elements is immensely varied. But amidst that variety there are patterns, and the best known and most useful is chemical periodicity: if the elements are laid out in order of atomic number, similar elements occur at regular intervals.

3.1 Chemical periodicity

The discovery of chemical periodicity is particularly associated with the nineteenth-century Russian chemist Dmitri Ivanovich Mendeléev (Figure 3.1). The periodicity is represented graphically by Periodic Tables. Figure 3.2 shows the Periodic Table used in S205. Chemical periodicity is apparent from the appearance of similar elements in the same column. For example, the alkali metals appear in the first column on the left of the Table, and the noble gases in the last column on the right. Horizontal rows are called *Periods*; vertical columns are called *Groups*. The Table can be neatly divided up into blocks of elements (transition elements, lanthanides, actinides and typical elements), each with their own distinctive properties. Above each element is its atomic number. These numbers run from 1–118, 118 being the highest atomic number so far [2001] claimed for any observed atom.

Figure 3.1
The hypnotic face of Dmitri Mendeléev (1834–1907) has been likened to that of Svengali or Rasputin. Such comparisons are encouraged by his insistence on having just one haircut a year. His scientific fame rests mainly on his boldness in using his Periodic Law to predict the properties of undiscovered elements. For example, after Lecoq de Boisbaudron had announced the discovery of the new element gallium in 1875, he received a letter from Mendeléev. The letter informed him that Mendeléev had already predicted the properties of gallium, and that his experimental value for its density appeared to be wrong. de Boisbaudron then redetermined the density of gallium, and found that Mendeléev's assertion was indeed correct!

S205 is largely concerned with the typical elements. These occur on the extreme left and extreme right of Figure 3.2. It is convenient, therefore, to create from Figure 3.2 a mini-Periodic Table that contains the typical elements alone. By removing the transition elements, the lanthanides and actinides, and by pushing the two separate blocks of typical elements together, we arrive at Figure 3.3. This mini-Periodic Table consists of seven Periods and eight Groups. The seven Periods are numbered from 1 to 7, but it is more difficult to settle on the best way of labelling the Groups.

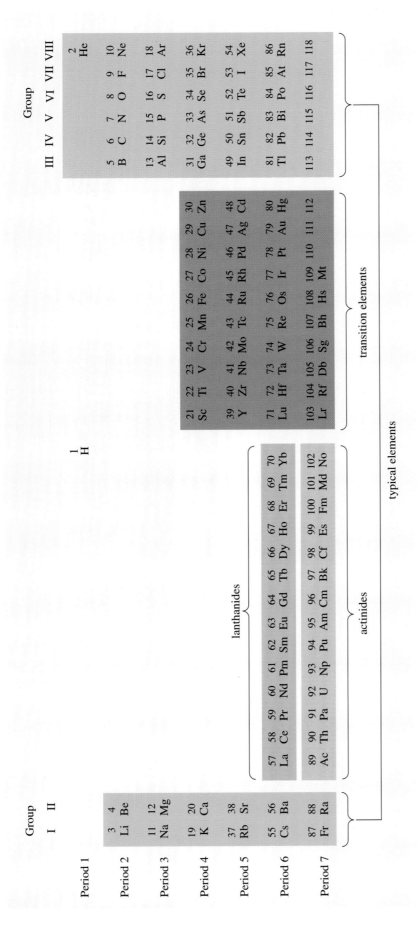

Figure 3.2 The complete Periodic Table used in S205. Note how the position of hydrogen has been left undecided. Some of its properties point to a position in Group I with the alkali metals; others to a position in Group VII with the halogens.

In Figure 3.3, they are numbered in roman numerals from I to VIII. This is the principal Group numbering scheme used in S205, but other ways of numbering the Groups are mentioned in Sections 3.2 and 3.3.

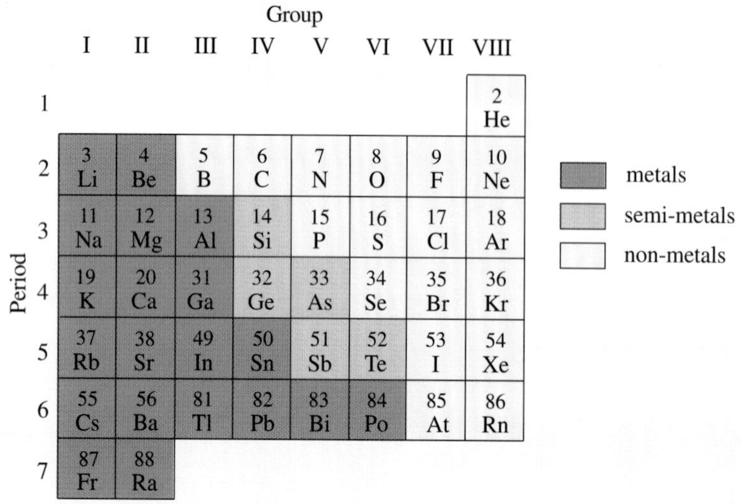

Figure 3.3
A mini-Periodic Table containing the typical elements up to radium; it consists of eight columns or Groups, and seven rows or Periods. Hydrogen has been omitted for the reasons cited in the caption to Figure 3.2.

Clear examples of chemical periodicity are revealed by Figure 3.3. Many involve the *valencies* of the elements. Here we use valency in the classical sense: a number that determines the ratios in which atoms combine. Table 3.1 shows the most important valencies of some common elements.

Table 3.1 The most important valencies of some common elements

Valency			
1	2	3	4
hydrogen (H)	oxygen (O)	nitrogen (N)	carbon (C)
lithium (Li)	sulfur (S)	phosphorus (P)	silicon (Si)
sodium (Na)	magnesium (Mg)	aluminium (Al)	tin (Sn)
potassium (K)	calcium (Ca)		
fluorine (F)	barium (Ba)		
chlorine (Cl)			
bromine (Br)			
iodine (I)			

◯ What does Table 3.1 suggest for the empirical formula of an oxide of tin?

◯ SnO_2; we start with the valencies of tin (4) and oxygen (2). Exchanging the numbers against the elements gives us tin (2) and oxygen (4). This tells us the combining ratio: two tin atoms combine with four oxygen atoms. To get the empirical formula, the ratio $2:4$ is converted to the lowest possible whole numbers; the result is $1:2$. So the predicted formula of the oxide of tin is SnO_2.

We now list three instances of chemical periodicity in Figure 3.3 that you should be able to exploit:

(i) As the colour coding of Figure 3.3 shows, metals lie to the left, and non-metals to the right, with semi-metals in between.

(ii) When an element in Figure 3.3 forms one or more hydrides, then across the eight columns of the Table, the valency of the element in the highest hydride (the hydride that contains most hydrogen) runs in the order 1, 2, 3, 4, 3, 2, 1, 0. Thus, nitrogen occurs in the fifth column, so its hydride is NH_3 (ammonia).

(iii) In the fluorides and normal oxides* of most of the elements in Figure 3.3, the highest observed valencies are equal to the Group number of the element. This allows the empirical formulae of the highest fluorides and highest normal oxides of the elements to be predicted. Thus, aluminium occurs in Group III, so the highest fluoride is AlF_3, and the highest normal oxide is Al_2O_3.

These generalizations are not perfect. For example, the oxide trend does not work for the elements Po, F, Br, I, He, Ne, Ar, Kr and Rn; the fluoride trend does not work for N, O, Cl, Br, or for any of the noble gases. Nevertheless, each generalization is true enough to be useful, and in S205, parts of Book 9 will be concerned with an understanding of the exceptions.

3.2 The Group number of the noble gases

In Figure 3.3, the Period numbers increase steadily from 1 to 7 down the columns. It obviously seems appropriate that the Group numbers should show a similar steady increase from I to VIII across the rows. However, this numbering scheme puts the noble gases in Group VIII. As Section 3.1 makes clear, almost none of these six elements then obeys generalization (iii). For example, with this Group numbering, generalization (iii) predicts the formula AO_4 for the highest normal oxides of the noble gases, where A represents a noble gas atom. Only for xenon is such a compound known.

The situation is improved if one changes the Group number of the noble gases from VIII to zero. This is because there are no known oxides or binary fluorides of helium, neon or argon. In the case of the noble gases, generalization (iii) then fails only at xenon when predicting oxide formulae, and at krypton, xenon and radon when predicting fluoride formulae. So in introducing chemical periodicity through generalizations (ii) and (iii), it makes sense to number the first 7 Groups from I to VII as in Figure 3.3, but to use zero for the noble gases (Group 0). This numbering is used, for example, on the CD-ROM associated with this Book, in which chemical periodicity is introduced in this way. It was also the Group numbering favoured by Mendeléev. In S205, however, we shall use the scheme of Figure 3.3 in which the noble gases are designated as Group VIII, and the Group numbers increase regularly across each row. The reasons for this change are given in Section 4.3.

---

* **Normal oxides** are compounds in which *single oxygen atoms* are combined with atoms of other elements. This distinguishes them from *peroxides* and *superoxides* (Book 4), in which two oxygen atoms are joined in pairs, similar to the situation in the O_2 molecule.

3.3 An alternative Group numbering scheme for the typical elements

You will often find the Groups of the typical elements numbered in a way that differs from that shown in Figure 3.3. This numbering scheme is described on the section of the CD-ROM programme *Surveying the Periodic Table* entitled 'An alternative Periodic Table'. It leads to a situation in which the eight group numbers of Figure 3.3 become 1, 2, 13, 14, 15, 16, 17 and 18 across a row. Thus, the carbon group, which is Group IV in Figure 3.3, becomes Group 14. The disadvantages of this scheme are especially obvious when dealing with the chemistry of the typical elements. Whereas, for example, the number four is equal to the valencies of carbon and silicon, and to the number of outer electrons in their atoms, the number 14 bears no relationship whatever to any physical or chemical property of the elements carbon and silicon. Nevertheless, this scheme is often used in chemical research journals, so you should be aware of it. In Book 9, we shall remind you of it by including it as an alternative in the headings under which each Group is treated. Thus, the carbon group will be written Group IV/14.

3.4 Summary of Section 3

1   The typical elements can be displayed in a mini-Periodic Table of eight Groups and seven Periods (Figure 3.3). The Periods are numbered from 1 to 7 and the Groups are labelled I–VIII.

2   Metals appear on the left of this table, non-metals on the right and semi-metals in between.

3   In their highest fluorides and normal oxides, the valencies of the typical elements are usually equal to their Group numbers in Figure 3.3. In their highest hydrides, their valencies usually follow the pattern 1, 2, 3, 4, 3, 2, 1, 0 across the Period.

QUESTION 3.1

A typical element Z from Figure 3.3 is a semi-metal and forms oxides with empirical formulae ZO_2 and ZO_3, and a single hydride, ZH_2. Identify the element, and state the Group and Period of Figures 3.3 in which it lies. What is the formula of the highest fluoride of the element?

STUDY NOTE

If you wish to revise the periodic properties discussed in Section 3 more fully, view the typical element section of the programme *Surveying the Periodic Table* on the CD-ROM associated with this Book. The CD-ROM also contains additional problems of the type dealt with in Question 3.1.

CHEMISTRY CAN OFTEN BE EXPLAINED BY ELECTRONIC STRUCTURE

4

Section 3 used some simple examples to illustrate chemical periodicity. But how can we explain such periodicity? The answer lies in the way that the electrons in atoms are arranged about the positively charged nucleus. In chemical reactions, atoms change partners. We know that the outsides of atoms consist of electrons, so contact and connection between atoms is likely to take place through their electrons, and in particular, through the electrons in their outer shells. *So similarities in the arrangement of the outer electrons in the atoms of two different elements lead to similarities in the chemistry of the two elements*. To see the truth of this idea, you must be able to write down the electronic configurations of atoms.

4.1 The electronic configurations of atoms

The quantum theory of the atom tells us that we cannot say exactly where an electron in an atom will be at any particular moment; we can speak only of the *probability* of finding an electron at a particular point. So the precise orbits shown in the Rutherford model of Figure 2.1 misrepresent the arrangement of electrons about the nucleus. We say instead that the electrons in atoms are arranged around the nucleus in shells. The shells are regions where the probability of finding an electron is relatively high, and where, over an extended period, the electrons spend most of their time. Shells are numbered 1, 2, 3, etc., starting from 1 nearest the nucleus. This number is called the *principal quantum number*, and is given the symbol n.

Now these shells of electrons can be divided into sub-shells, and each sub-shell is specified by a second quantum number l.

● How many sub-shells are there in a shell of principal quantum number 4? Assign an l value to each sub-shell.

● There are four. For a shell of principal quantum number n, l can take values from zero up to $(n - 1)$. Thus, in the shell for which $n = 4$, there are four sub-shells with the values $l = 0, 1, 2$ and 3.

An alternative way of specifying sub-shells uses letters in place of the quantum number l. The following letters are used in this notation: s for sub-shells with $l = 0$, p for sub-shells with $l = 1$, d for sub-shells with $l = 2$, f for sub-shells with $l = 3$. Thus, the four sub-shells in the shell for which $n = 4$ are written 4s, 4p, 4d and 4f.

There is an *upper limit* on the number of electrons that each kind of sub-shell can hold. This limit is $2(2l + 1)$, where l is the second quantum number of the sub-shell.

● What is this upper limit for each of the s, p, d and f sub-shells?

● The values are: $2[(2 \times 0) + 1] = 2$; $2[(2 \times 1) + 1] = 6$; $2[(2 \times 2) + 1] = 10$; and $2[(2 \times 3) + 1] = 14$, respectively.

So in s, p, d and f sub-shells, there can be no more than 2, 6, 10 and 14 electrons, respectively. These limits, and other quantum rules from this Section are summarized in Figure 4.1.

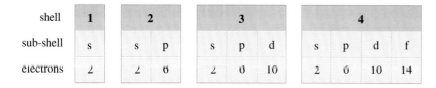

shell	1	2		3			4			
sub-shell	s	s	p	s	p	d	s	p	d	f
electrons	2	2	6	2	6	10	2	6	10	14

Figure 4.1 The sub-shells in the shells of principal quantum numbers 1–4, and the maximum number of electrons that each type of sub-shell can hold.

To assign electronic configurations to atoms, you need only one more piece of information. This is an energy-level diagram displaying the order in which the sub-shells are filled. Surprisingly, electronic configurations can be correctly assigned to *nearly all* atoms using just one such diagram, Figure 4.2.

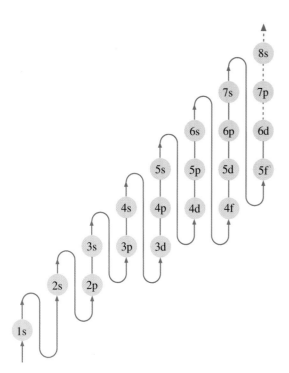

Figure 4.2
A pathway showing the order in which the sub-shells should be filled when writing out the electronic configurations of atoms.

The atomic number of silicon is 14. Write down the electronic configuration of the silicon atom.

$1s^2 2s^2 2p^6 3s^2 3p^2$.

This is established as follows. Assign the fourteen electrons in the silicon atom to the sub-shells in Figure 4.2. The 1s and 2s levels on the left can each take two electrons. The next highest level is 2p and this sub-shell is filled by the next six electrons. The 3s sub-shell then takes another two electrons and the thirteenth and fourteenth electrons go into the sub-shell of next highest energy, which is 3p.

Notice that the value of n for the outermost shell of the electronic configuration of the silicon atom is three. This outer shell contains four electrons, two of which are in an s sub-shell, and two in a p sub-shell. We say, therefore, that the outer electronic configuration of the silicon atom is of the type s^2p^2.

4.2 Electronic configurations and the Periodic Table

Figure 4.2 has been designed for use in a particular *thought experiment*. The purpose of the thought experiment is to see how the electronic configuration of the atoms *changes* as one moves through the Periodic Table from beginning to end. We start with the hydrogen atom, which has one proton and one electron. Then we proceed through a series of stages in each of which we add one new proton to the nucleus, and one new electron to the clutch of surrounding electrons. At each stage, the filling order of Figure 4.2 tells us what sub-shells are occupied, and how many electrons those occupied sub-shells contain. In addition, the filling of successive sub-shells in this thought experiment generates the form of the Periodic Table shown in Figure 4.3, in which the winding arrowed pathway follows the filling order of Figure 4.2. The different blocks of elements span regions in which particular types of sub-shells are being filled up. With the typical elements, the sub-shell type is either s or p; in the case of the transition elements, with rows of ten, it is d; for the lanthanides and actinides, with rows of fourteen, it is f. Indeed, because of this connection, one can think of Figure 4.3 as a demonstration of how the filling order of Figure 4.2 can be deduced from the form of the Periodic Table.

4.2.1 Writing out electronic configurations

In Section 4.1, we described Figure 4.2 as an *energy-level* diagram, which represented the build-up of electronic configurations as electrons were inserted into sub-shells of progressively increasing energy. However, Figure 4.2 has been designed for just one purpose: to generate the correct electronic configurations in our thought experiment in which, to quote Niels Bohr, 'the neutral atom is built up by the capture and binding of electrons to the nucleus, one by one'. What Figure 4.2 tells us, at any stage of the thought experiment, is which of the *still unfilled* sub-shells has the lowest energy. That sub-shell then receives the next electron.

Figure 4.2 is therefore designed to give the order of energies only for those sub-shells that, at any stage of the thought experiment, are candidates for the reception of the next electron. It does not necessarily give the correct order of energies for *all* of the sub-shells in any *one particular atom*. Consider lead, atomic number 82.

⬤ Use Figure 4.2 to write out the electronic configuration of the lead atom.

⬤ $1s^2 2s^2 2p^6 3s^2 3p^6 4s^2 3d^{10} 4p^6 5s^2 4d^{10} 5p^6 6s^2 4f^{14} 5d^{10} 6p^2$.

In the lead atom, the occupied sub-shells of highest energy are $6s^2$ and $6p^2$. The four electrons in these sub-shells are the ones that most influence the chemistry of lead. They are the outermost electrons, and the most easily removed, being furthest from the nucleus. But the sub-shell sequence from Figure 4.2 does not give this impression. Although $6p^2$ appears at the end, suggesting that these are outermost electrons, $6s^2$ does not. A more correct order of energies *in any particular atom* is

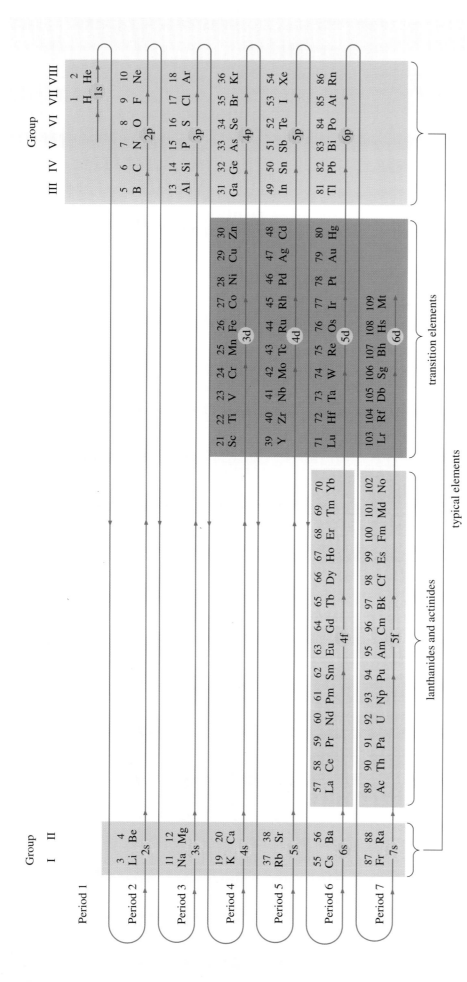

Figure 4.3 The winding pathway shows how the order of sub-shell filling (Figure 4.2) generates the full Periodic Table. Elements in the same column *usually* have similar outer electronic configurations. Hydrogen has been juxtaposed with helium to indicate the filling of the 1s sub-shell.

obtained by grouping the sub-shells first in order of increasing value of n, and then, within each n value, in the order s, p, d and f.

⬤ Do this for the configuration of the lead atom.

⬤ $1s^2|2s^22p^6|3s^23p^63d^{10}|4s^24p^64d^{10}4f^{14}|5s^25p^65d^{10}|6s^26p^2$. For clarification, the individual shells have been separated by vertical lines.

The electronic configurations of the atoms in the S205 *Data Book* have been written in this style. One of its merits is that the outer electrons with the highest principal quantum numbers appear at the right-hand end. In this case, they show that the outer electronic configuration of lead is of the type s^2p^2. This is less apparent in the earlier configuration that was derived directly from Figure 4.2.

4.3 Outer electronic configurations and the Periodic Table

The essential message of Figure 4.3 is that the Groups of elements that appear in columns of the Periodic Table usually have atoms with similar outer electronic configurations. Figure 4.4 incorporates these configurations into our mini-Periodic Table of typical elements; they appear at the top of each Group. They imply that the typical elements have outer electronic configurations either of the type ns^x, where $x = 1$ or 2, or of the type ns^2np^x, where x runs from 1 to 6. For any particular element, n is the principal quantum number of the outer occupied shell. This can easily be found from Figure 4.4, because it is equal to the number of the Period in which the element is to be found. The outer electrons are simply those in occupied sub-shells with this principal quantum number.

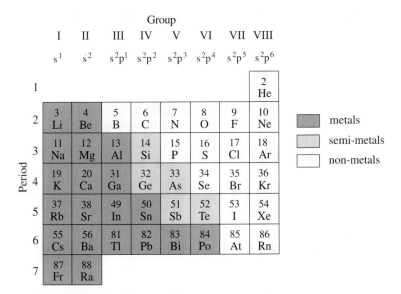

Figure 4.4 A mini-Periodic Table for the typical elements up to radium. Along the top are the Group numbers in roman numerals, and the outer electronic configurations of the elements of each Group. As in Figure 3.3, hydrogen has been omitted.

⬤ According to Figure 4.4, what are the principal quantum numbers of the outer occupied shells for the atoms of silicon and lead?

⬤ Three and six, respectively: silicon appears in Period 3 and lead in Period 6.

According to Figure 4.4 therefore, silicon and lead have outer electronic configurations of the type ns^2np^2, with $n = 3$ for silicon and $n = 6$ for lead. This is just what you got when you worked out the full electronic configuration of the silicon and lead atoms in Sections 4.1 and 4.2.1, respectively.

⬤ According to Figure 4.4, what is the relationship between the Group number for silicon and lead, and the outer electronic configurations of their atoms?

⬤ In both cases, the Group number is four and there are four outer electrons: two s electrons and two p electrons.

Here is confirmation of the explanation of chemical periodicity mentioned at the beginning of Section 4. Elements in the same Group of the Periodic Table behave similarly because they usually have similar outer electronic configurations. It also demonstrates that, for the typical elements, the total number of outer electrons is equal to the Group number. It is to preserve this generalization that, in S205, we take the Group number of the noble gases to be VIII rather than zero. Apart from helium ($1s^2$), they have eight outer electrons (s^2p^6).

Finally, notice that Figures 3.2 and 4.3 imply that the atoms of highest known atomic number (113–118) at the outer limit of the Periodic Table are expected to be typical elements. This is only one of the reasons that makes them of special interest (see Box 4.1 *The island of stability*).

4.4 Electron states and box diagrams

So far, we have represented the electronic state of an atom as a collection of sub-shells. Now we turn to the states of the electrons within those sub-shells. Just as shells can be broken down into sub-shells, so sub-shells can be broken down into **atomic orbitals**. Each atomic orbital describes an allowed spatial distribution about the nucleus for an electron in the sub-shell. You will learn more about these distributions in Book 6. Here we shall only be concerned with their number.

Consider the formula for the sub-shell electron capacities, which is $2(2l + 1)$, l being the second quantum number. The factor $(2l + 1)$ tells us the number of atomic orbitals in the sub-shell.

⬤ How many atomic orbitals are there in an s sub-shell, and how many in a p sub-shell?

⬤ One and three, respectively; for s and p sub-shells, $l = 0$ and 1, so $(2l + 1) = 1$ and 3, respectively.

It turns out that each orbital in a sub-shell can contain up to two electrons. This is connected to a property of the electron called **spin**. This spin occurs in one of two senses, which are physically pictured as clockwise and anticlockwise (Figure 4.5).

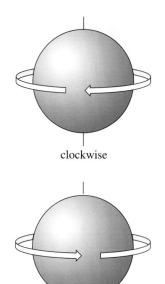

clockwise

anticlockwise

Figure 4.5
The two senses of electron spin.

BOX 4.1   The island of stability

The elements of highest atomic number are made through the collision of atoms and ions of lighter elements in particle accelerators. Success does not come easily, because the atoms that are formed are highly radioactive and very short lived. However, theory suggests that somewhere above atomic number 110 there is an 'island of stability', where the atoms will have longer lifetimes. This island is marked by favourable combinations of neutrons and protons, with its summit centred around an atom of atomic number 114 and mass number 298. So far [2001], the elements of highest atomic number for which isotopes have been identified are 114, 116 and 118. These may therefore supply evidence for the existence of the island.

In 1999, scientists at Dubna in Russia made the first atoms of element 114, to which we shall give the provisional name auditorium (Ad)! Ions of the isotope $^{48}_{20}Ca$ were accelerated to $30\,000\ km\,h^{-1}$, and directed on to a target containing the plutonium isotope $^{244}_{94}Pu$. Two nuclei fused, three neutrons were ejected, and an atom of the 289 isotope of element 114 was produced:

$$^{48}_{20}Ca + ^{244}_{94}Pu \longrightarrow ^{289}_{114}Ad + 3^{1}_{0}n$$

The half-life of $^{289}_{114}Ad$ proved to be 30 seconds. It underwent α-decay to the 285 isotope of element 112, whose half-life is 15.4 minutes. These half-lives may seem short, but you must go back to element 103 to find known isotopes which are as long lived.

Figure 4.6* shows the half-lives of the known isotopes of elements 112–118. $^{289}_{114}Ad$ and the two other isotopes of element 114 support the emergence of an island of stability, but we are still a long way (9 neutrons) from the predicted summit at 184 neutrons. There is a reason for this. The proportion of neutrons in the most stable isotope of an element increases with atomic number. So the lighter isotopes such as $^{48}_{20}Ca$ and $^{244}_{94}Pu$, from which the new heavy elements are made, lack the neutrons needed to produce the *most stable* isotope of the heavier element that they create.

This is simultaneously encouraging and discouraging. It means that the expected summit of the island of stability will be hard to reach. But if we do get there, we may find very stable elements. It may even be possible to study their chemistry. In Book 9, we shall try to predict what this might be like.

* Recent [2001] research has shown that experimental difficulties make results of the type summarized in Figure 4.6 more subject to change than most scientific data. The claim by workers at Berkeley, California that they had prepared an isotope of element 118 has now been withdrawn. However, the Russian group at Dubna believes that it has successfully made atoms of the 292 isotope of element 116 with a half life of 0.05 s.

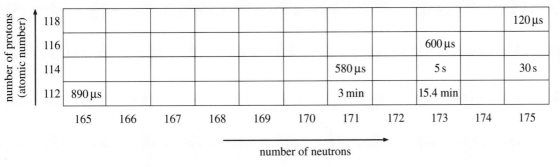

number of protons (atomic number)	165	166	167	168	169	170	171	172	173	174	175	
118											120 µs	
116									600 µs			
114							580 µs		5 s		30 s	to the summit (9 neutrons)
112	890 µs						3 min		15.4 min			

number of neutrons

Figure 4.6 As the number of neutrons in known isotopes of each of the elements 112–118 increases above 165, the half-lives increase (even-numbered elements only shown). This indicates the emergence of an island of stability whose summit is predicted to be at 114 protons and 184 neutrons. (1 µs = 10^{-6} s; 1 min = 1 minute)

When an atomic orbital contains its maximum complement of two electrons, those two electrons must always have spins of opposite sense. This phenomenon of electron spin accounts for the '2' that precedes the bracket in the formula for sub-shell capacities, $2(2l + 1)$. For example, as we have seen, the factor $(2l + 1)$ tells us that there are three atomic orbitals in a p sub-shell. Each of the three orbitals can accommodate up to two electrons with opposed spins. So a p sub-shell can contain a maximum of 2×3 or 6 electrons.

A full atomic orbital, therefore, contains two electrons with spins of opposite sense. This is represented by writing one electron as an upward-pointing half-headed arrow, and the other as a downward-pointing half-headed arrow. For example, the helium atom has the electronic configuration $1s^2$. The 1s sub-shell contains just one orbital, which can be represented by a single box containing the two electrons of opposite spin:

↑↓

1s

Two such electrons with opposed spins are said to be *paired* and the diagram that puts these electrons into boxes is referred to as a **box diagram**. Now consider the case of nitrogen, whose atom has the configuration $1s^2 2s^2 2p^3$. The 1s and 2s sub-shells contain one orbital each, and the 2p sub-shell contains three. The box diagram that must be filled therefore takes the form:

  1s   2s   2p

●   Assign the two 1s and two 2s electrons of nitrogen to boxes in this diagram.

●   The 1s and 2s boxes should now both look like the 1s box for the helium atom above: they should each contain two electrons with opposed spins.

The final step is the assignment of the three 2p electrons to the three 2p boxes. There are several possibilities, but the one we want is the **ground-state** arrangement, the state of lowest energy. There is a simple rule, called **Hund's rule**, that tells us what this is:

> Within any sub-shell, there will be the maximum number of electrons with spins of the same sense.

Because electrons in the same box must have opposed spins, we must put the electrons, as far as possible, in different boxes with spins of the same sense, or, as it is usually termed, with **parallel spins**. In this case there are three 2p electrons and three boxes, so each box can take one electron with the same spin, and this is the preferred arrangement according to Hund's rule. The final result for the nitrogen atom is therefore:

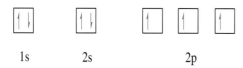

  1s   2s   2p

○ The oxygen atom, with the configuration $1s^2 2s^2 2p^4$, has one more electron than the nitrogen atom. Draw the box diagram for the oxygen atom.

○ As there are four 2p electrons and only three 2p boxes, the fourth 2p electron cannot have a spin parallel to the other three. It must go into a box that is already occupied by one electron with opposite spin:

1s   2s   2p

4.5 Summary of Section 4

1   The electronic configuration of an atom can be obtained by allocating its electrons to s, p, d and f sub-shells in the order given by Figure 4.2. This procedure generates a periodicity in electronic configuration which matches that of the Periodic Table.

2   The typical elements have outer electronic configurations of the type ns^x, where $x = 1$ or 2, or of the type $ns^2 np^x$, where x runs from 1 to 6, and n, the principal quantum number, is equal to the number of the Period.

3   In Figure 4.4, the Group numbers are equal to the number of outer electrons, except in the case of helium.

4   The ground (electronic) state of an atom can be represented by a box diagram in which each sub-shell of the electronic configuration is broken down into atomic orbitals. Each orbital is portrayed as a box that can accommodate up to two electrons with opposite spins. In incomplete sub-shells, the electrons are assigned to the boxes so as to maximize the number of parallel spins (Hund's rule).

QUESTION 4.1

Use Figure 4.4 to identify the elements whose outer electronic configurations are (a) $3s^2 3p^5$; (b) $4s^2 4p^3$; (c) $6s^2 6p^1$.

QUESTION 4.2

Write down the electronic configurations of (a) the calcium atom (atomic number 20); (b) the bromine atom (atomic number 35); and (c) the tin atom (atomic number 50). Make sure you order the sub-shells according to their principal atomic number.

QUESTION 4.3

Substance A is both a typical element and a metal. It forms two normal oxides, A_2O_3 and A_2O_5, and two fluorides AF_3 and AF_5. Identify A, and state its outer electronic configuration.

QUESTION 4.4

Represent the electronic ground state of the chlorine atom by a box diagram.

CHEMICAL BONDS CONSIST OF SHARED PAIRS OF ELECTRONS

5

Simple theories of chemical bonding are based on the idea of the electron-pair bond, and the extent to which the electron pair is shared between the bound atoms. There is also an assumption that the electronic structures of noble gas atoms are especially stable, and that many elements try to attain these structures when they react to form chemical compounds. These ideas were the brainchild of the American chemist, G. N. Lewis (Box 5.1). In developing them, we shall simplify the electronic configurations of atoms by writing *shell structures* that merely show the electron content of successive shells. Shell structures for atoms of elements 2–20 are shown in Figure 5.2.

BOX 5.1 G. N. Lewis

Until he was 14, Gilbert Newton Lewis (1875–1946; Figure 5.1) was educated at home in Nebraska by his parents. It is remarkable that he did not win a Nobel Prize, because, as J. W. Linnett, sometime Professor of Physical Chemistry at Cambridge said, his idea of the electron-pair bond is 'the most productive and important contribution that has ever been made to the subject of valency and chemical binding'. In 1912, he became Chairman of a rather lacklustre chemistry department at the University of Berkeley in California. He set about reorganizing and revitalizing the department, appointing staff

with a broad chemical knowledge rather than specalists. Under his direction, it quickly acquired the world reputation that it still enjoys today. During the First World War, he trained gas warfare specialists and was made a Lieutenant-Colonel. A love of cigars may have contributed to his death from heart failure while doing an experiment.

Figure 5.1 G. N. Lewis.

							He 2
Li 2,1	Be 2,2	B 2,3	C 2,4	N 2,5	O 2,6	F 2,7	Ne 2,8
Na 2,8,1	Mg 2,8,2	Al 2,8,3	Si 2,8,4	P 2,8,5	S 2,8,6	Cl 2,8,7	Ar 2,8,8
K 2,8,8,1	Ca 2,8,8,2						

Figure 5.2
A part Periodic Table showing shell structures for atoms of elements 2–20.

5.1 Ionic and covalent bonding

We begin by applying simple bonding theories to molecular chlorine gas (Cl_2) and non-molecular sodium chloride (NaCl), whose structures were discussed in Section 2. Figure 5.3 shows the result.

Figure 5.3a shows the **Lewis structure** of the Cl_2 molecule. Note that the electrons are grouped in pairs. This reflects the pairing of electrons in atomic orbitals noted in Section 4.4. The ions in sodium chloride have also been represented in this way in Figure 5.3b. The chloride ion has the shell structure of argon, with eight outer electrons, and the electron transferred from the sodium atom is marked by a small filled circle. In both structures, the formation of a chemical bond involves the production of a new electron pair in the outer shell of chlorine. However, in Cl_2, because the two atoms are identical, the electron pair must be equally shared between the two atoms; in NaCl by contrast, it resides on the resulting chloride ion.

From this contrast flows the difference in properties between the two substances. The transference of the electron to chlorine in NaCl produces ions, each of which can exist independently of any one partner. So in sodium chloride, each ion is surrounded by as many ions of opposite charge as space allows. In this case the number is six, as you saw in Figure 2.10. Figure 5.4 is Figure 2.10 adjusted to show the presence of ions. Because of the strong attractive forces existing between the closely packed ions of opposite charge, the sodium chloride structure is not easily broken down: it has a high melting temperature and does not dissolve in organic solvents like the liquid hydrocarbons found in petrol, or dry-cleaning fluid. When it does melt, or dissolve in water, the ions separate and the resulting ionic fluid conducts electricity. Compounds of this type are called *ionic*, and the type of bonding is called *ionic bonding*.

By contrast, in Cl_2, the electron pair is shared. This is called *covalent bonding*. Here, the bonding can be maintained only if the atoms stay together in pairs, so it gives rise to a molecular substance: elemental chlorine consists of discrete Cl_2 molecules with only weak forces acting between them. It is a gas at room temperature, and dissolves easily in liquid hydrocarbons, including petrol. However, because a solution of chlorine contains no ions, it does not conduct electricity.

⦿ According to this picture, ionic and covalent bonding are the same process carried to different extents; what is the process, and how do the extents differ?

⦿ The common process is the formation of an electron-pair bond; in covalent bonding the electron pair is shared between the atoms involved; in ionic bonding it resides on just one of them.

This link between ionic and covalent bonding is clarified by the concept of *electronegativity*. The electronegativity of an element is a measure of the power of its atom to attract electrons to itself *when forming chemical bonds*. In the Cl_2 molecule, the two identical atoms have an equal appetite for electrons: their electronegativities are equal, so the electron pair is shared equally between them. Now consider sodium chloride.

⦿ Which atom is the more electronegative, sodium or chlorine?

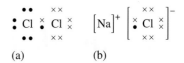

(a)   (b)

Figure 5.3
Lewis structures for (a) gaseous Cl_2 and (b) solid NaCl. Chlorine has seven outer electrons, but can acquire an additional electron to give eight, and the shell structure of argon, if an electron pair is shared between the two atoms in Cl_2. Sodium has one outer electron, so sodium can acquire a neon shell, and chlorine an argon shell structure if this electron is transferred to a chlorine atom. This generates the Na^+ and Cl^- ions in sodium chloride.

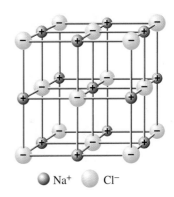

⬤ Na^+ ◯ Cl^-

Figure 5.4
An ionic picture of solid sodium chloride which explains important properties of the substance. The solid is regarded as an assembly of Na^+ and Cl^- ions.

In sodium chloride, the electron pair has been completely taken over by chlorine, which forms a chloride ion. Imagine the sodium and chlorine atoms competing for electrons; the chlorine atoms win, so chlorine is the more electronegative.

So chlorine, near the end of Period 3, has a greater electronegativity than sodium, at the beginning. This contrast applies generally: the electronegativities of atoms increase across a Period of the Periodic Table; electronegativities also usually increase up a Group from the bottom to the top. These trends are explained in Figure 5.5. More sophisticated ways of establishing electronegativities are discussed in Book 9.

atomic number increases

electronegativity tends to increase

3 Li	4 Be	5 B	6 C	7 N	8 O	9 F
11 Na	12 Mg	13 Al	14 Si	15 P	16 S	17 Cl
19 K	20 Ca	31 Ga	32 Ge	33 As	34 Se	35 Br
37 Rb	38 Sr	49 In	50 Sn	51 Sb	52 Te	53 I
55 Cs	56 Ba	81 Tl	82 Pb	83 Bi	84 Po	85 At
87 Fr	88 Ra					

principal quantum number of outer electrons decreases

electronegativity tends to increase

Figure 5.5 Across a Period of the Periodic Table, the atomic number, or positive charge on the nucleus, increases. This increases the attraction of the outer electrons to the nucleus, so the electronegativity of the elements also increases. The principal quantum number of the outer electrons decreases from the bottom to the top of a Group. This means that they get closer to the positively charged nucleus. The result is, again, that the outer electrons are attracted more strongly, and the electronegativity usually increases. The three most electronegative elements are shown on a green background.

Figure 5.5 shows that the most electronegative elements lie towards the top right-hand corner of the Periodic Table. Electronegativities refer to an attraction for outer electrons when an element is forming compounds. The noble gases have been omitted from Figure 5.5 because at normal temperatures helium, neon and argon form no compounds; hence electronegativities are not assigned to them. Consequently, fluorine is the most electronegative element, followed by oxygen and chlorine.

Figure 5.5 confirms that chlorine is much more electronegative than sodium. Because of this large difference in electronegativity, the electron pair ($\overset{\times}{_{\bullet}}$) of Figure 5.3b spends all its time on chlorine, the charges on sodium and chlorine are +1 and −1, respectively, and NaCl is ionic. So the electronegativity trends in Figure 5.5 explain why ionic compounds arise when a metallic element of low electronegativity from the left of the Periodic Table combines with a non-metallic element of high electronegativity from the right. In Cl_2, by contrast, the electronegativity difference between the bound elements is zero; the shared electrons spend equal times on each chlorine atom, both chlorines are uncharged, the substance is molecular, and is held together by covalent bonding. Covalently bound molecular substances such as Cl_2, I_2 and CO_2 (Section 2.3) are combinations from the right of Figure 5.5, because, although for these elements the individual electronegativities are large, the electronegativity *differences* between them are small.

These two cases deal with combinations of elements with very different electronegativities from the left and right of Figure 5.5 (ionic bonding), and with combinations of elements of high but similar electronegativity from the right (covalent bonding). But what is the result of combining elements of low but similar electronegativity from the left? The reasoning that we have pursued until now suggests that, in this case, electronegativity differences between atoms will be small, so again we would expect shared electron-pair bonds and covalent substances, possibly of the molecular type typified by Cl_2.

- Is this correct? Answer by considering what happens when sodium atoms become bound together at room temperature.

- It is incorrect; at room temperature, sodium atoms do not yield Na_2 molecules. Instead, they form a non-molecular metal.

So let us look more closely at the bonding in metals.

5.2 Metallic bonding

Two familiar properties of metals point to a simple model of metallic bonding. Firstly, metals have a strong tendency to form positive ions. Thus, when sodium reacts with water, and when magnesium and aluminium react with acids, hydrogen gas is evolved and the ions $Na^+(aq)$, $Mg^{2+}(aq)$ and $Al^{3+}(aq)$, respectively, are formed. Secondly, metals are good conductors of electricity: when a voltage difference is applied across two points on a piece of metal, there is a movement of electrons between the two points, and an electric current flows.

Figure 5.6 exploits these two observations to produce a model of the bonding in a metal like sodium. The sodium sites in the metallic crystal are assumed to be occupied by Na^+ ions with the shell structure of neon. The Na^+ ions are formed by removing the single outer electrons from each sodium atom. The electrons so removed are no longer tied to individual sodium sites, and are allowed to move freely throughout the entire volume of the metallic substance. These free electrons, sometimes described as an '**electron gas**', are responsible for a metal's ability to conduct electricity. At the same time, they occupy the space between the positive sodium ions, so their negative charge acts like a binding glue pulling the sodium sites together.

So electron-sharing has taken place as predicted at the end of Section 5.1, but in a different way: because all the atoms have low electronegativities, they are prepared to surrender electrons to other atoms, either by electron transfer or electron-pair sharing. However, the low electronegativities mean that none of the atoms present will readily *take on* these electrons, either by forming a negative ion, or by accepting a share in electron-pair bonds. Consequently, a pool of free electrons

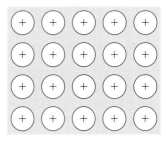

Figure 5.6
In the electron gas model of metallic bonding for metals and alloys, an array of positive ions is steeped in a pool of negatively charged free electrons (indicated by the background blue tone). The electrons pull the positive ions together.

is created which is like hot money: they are passed quickly from hand to hand, and can find no permanent home! This is the situation pictured in Figure 5.6. So far in this Section, we have only considered cases where all the combining atoms are the same, and a metallic *element* is the result. However, such metallic substances can be formed from two or more elements, and they are then called **alloys**.

5.3 A classification of chemical substances

We now have a provisional but useful classification of chemical substances. First they are divided into molecular and non-molecular types, largely on the basis of their structures. Then a further division is made according to the major source of the chemical bonding holding their atoms together. In molecular substances, the bonding is covalent, but in the non-molecular class, it may be covalent, ionic or metallic. This classification is shown in Figure 5.7. For a recent and interesting example of a substance changing categories within this classification, see Box 5.2, *Turning dry ice into sand*.

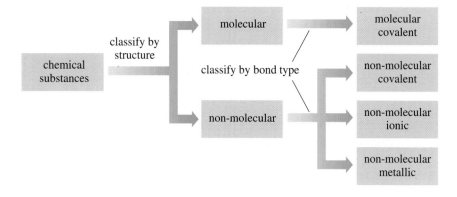

Figure 5.7
A classification of chemical substances using, first, structure, and then bond type, as criteria.

5.4 More about covalent bonding

So far, the valencies in Table 3.1 have just been numbers that we use to predict the formulae of compounds. But in the case of covalent substances they can tell us more. In particular, they can tell us how the atoms are linked together in the molecule. This information is obtained from a two-dimensional drawing of the **structural formula** of the molecule. (Note that structural formulae cannot be assumed to carry any implications about molecular shape.) Consider, for example, the molecules H_2, Cl_2, NCl_3 and CH_4. Their structural formulae are shown here as Structures **5.1–5.4**. They can be drawn correctly by ensuring that the number of lines or bonds emerging from any atom is equal to its valency. Thus, in Structure **5.3**, three bonds emerge from the nitrogen atom and one from each chlorine atom. The single lines of Structures **5.1–5.4** represent single bonds, but bonds may also be double or triple.

H—H

5.1

Cl—Cl

5.2

Cl—N—Cl
    |
    Cl

5.3

    H
    |
H—C—H
    |
    H

5.4

BOX 5.2 Turning dry ice into sand

As Mendeléev emphasized, the highest valencies of the elements are the clearest *chemical* sign of periodicity. At first glance, the highest oxides of carbon and silicon are quite different. CO_2 is a gas, which freezes to a molecular solid at −79 °C; SiO_2 is a non-molecular solid melting at over 1 500 °C. But despite these differences, both are *di*oxides. In both compounds, carbon and silicon exercise a valency of four, and this is why Mendeléev put both elements in the same Group.

Even the differences are not unalterable. In solid carbon dioxide (Figure 2.7), the distances between molecules are relatively large. The quartz structure of SiO_2 (Figure 2.11) is non-molecular, with identical short distances between neighbouring atoms. It is therefore more compact. When pressure is applied to a solid, it encourages a change into more compact forms. So at high pressures, solid CO_2 might shift to a silica-like structure. Raising the temperature should also help by speeding up any change.

In 1999, scientists at the Lawrence Livermore laboratory in California subjected solid carbon dioxide to 400 kilobars pressure. This is 400 times the pressure at the bottom of the Mariana Trench, the deepest point in the world's oceans. At these pressures, the CO_2 stayed solid even when the temperature was raised to 2 000 °C. The Livermore scientists then used a technique that you will meet in Book 8: they determined the Raman spectrum of the solid, a type of *vibrational spectrum*. It showed (Figure 5.8) that under these conditions the carbon dioxide had assumed a silica-like structure. Dry ice had taken on the structure of sand!

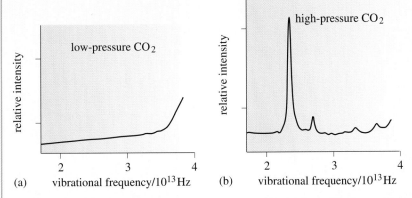

(a)   vibrational frequency/10^{13} Hz   (b)   vibrational frequency/10^{13} Hz

Figure 5.8 (a) At normal pressures, solid carbon dioxide is molecular, and its vibrational spectrum shows no peaks in the frequency range $2 \times 10^{13} - 4 \times 10^{13}$ Hz. (b) After heating at a pressure of 400 kilobars, a peak appears at 2.37×10^{13} Hz. This is characteristic of the vibrations of two carbon atoms bound to, and equidistant from, an oxygen atom. It suggests that solid CO_2 has assumed a silica-like form.

QUESTION 5.1

Check that you are comfortable with the bonding ideas discussed above by using the valencies of Table 3.1 to draw structural formulae for the following molecular substances: hydrogen chloride (HCl), ammonia (NH_3), water (H_2O), oxygen (O_2), carbon dioxide (CO_2), ethene (C_2H_4), hydrogen cyanide (HCN), ethyne (C_2H_2) and ethanal (CH_3CHO).

5.4.1 Lewis structures

G. N. Lewis used the shared electron-pair bond to re-express structural formulae in an electronic form. Examples appeared in Figure 5.3, where the sharing leads to Lewis structures in which each atom has the shell structure of a noble gas.

- Use the shell structures of Figure 5.2 to write down Lewis structures for (a) NH_3; (b) H_2O; (c) CO_2; (d) HCN.

- See Structures **5.5–5.8**; single, double and triple bonds are represented by one, two and three shared pairs of electrons, respectively. Hydrogen attains the shell structure of helium, with 2 outer electrons; carbon, nitrogen and oxygen attain that of neon, with 8 outer electrons.

5.5   5.6   5.7   5.8

Note that the electron pairs in these Lewis structures are of two types. The pairs shared between atoms represent chemical bonds and are called **bond pairs**. But there are also pairs that remain on just one atom and are unshared. These are called **non-bonded electron pairs** or **lone pairs**.

- How many bond pairs and non-bonded electron pairs are there in (a) the ammonia molecule; (b) the water molecule?

- NH_3 contains three bond pairs and one non-bonded pair. In H_2O there are two of each.

So far, we have only written Lewis structures for neutral molecules, but they can also be drawn for ions, such as the hydroxide ion, HO^- and the ammonium ion, NH_4^+. However, to take the charges into account we must begin by adding or subtracting electrons from particular atoms. To create a systematic procedure, we shall apply this process of addition or subtraction at the atom of highest valency. In HO^-, this is the oxygen atom; in NH_4^+, it is the nitrogen atom. As the hydroxide ion carries a single negative charge, we add one electron to the shell structure of the oxygen atom which is (2,6). This gives (2,7).

- What shell structure does a corresponding adjustment to the nitrogen atom in NH_4^+ generate?

- (2,4); the single positive charge on the ammonium ion requires the removal of one electron from the nitrogen atom shell structure, which is (2,5).

By allowing the ions O^- and N^+ to form single bonds to hydrogen atoms, we can generate Lewis structures for OH^- (Structure **5.9**) and NH_4^+ (Structure **5.10**) in which each atom has a noble gas electronic structure:

5.9   **5.10**

5.4.2 Noble gas configurations under stress

It is remarkable how many molecules and ions of the typical elements can be represented by Lewis structures in which each atom has a noble gas shell structure. Nevertheless, many exceptions exist. According to the periodic trends summarized in Section 3, the highest fluorides of boron and phosphorus are BF_3 and PF_5. However, phosphorus, in accordance with Table 3.1, also forms the lower fluoride PF_3. All three compounds are colourless gases at room temperature and contain the molecules BF_3, PF_3 and PF_5. As the valency of fluorine is one (Table 3.1), each bond in these molecules is a shared electron pair, and we may write the Lewis structures as follows:

5.11   **5.12**   **5.13**

● In how many of these Lewis structures do all the atoms have noble gas shell structures?

● In only one, namely that of PF_3; in Structure **5.11**, the three shared electron pairs around the boron atom are two electrons short of the shell structure of neon, and in Structure **5.13**, the five electron pairs around the phosphorus atom give us two electrons more than the shell structure of argon.

You will meet more exceptions of this sort in Section 7. Here, we merely note their existence, and observe that they are a consequence of our assumption that a chemical bond consists of *two* electrons shared between *two* atoms.

5.4.3 Dative bonds

So far, the bonds in our Lewis structures have been shared electron pairs made by taking one electron from each of the two bound atoms. But this need not necessarily be the case. In Sections 5.4.1 and 5.4.2, we encountered the colourless gases NH_3 and BF_3. When these gases are mixed, a solid compound H_3NBF_3 is formed as a dense white smoke. The chemical equation for the process is:

$$NH_3(g) + BF_3(g) = H_3NBF_3(s) \tag{5.1}$$

(The notation used in chemical equations is discussed in Box 5.3.)

BOX 5.3 Chemical equations and state symbols

Equation 5.1 is balanced. In S205, the two sides of balanced equations like this are connected by an equals sign, symbolizing the equality in the numbers of the different types of atom on each side. Unless otherwise stated, such equations should be understood as having a direction: they proceed from reactants on the left to products on the right. This is also true of the commonly used alternative to the equals sign — an arrow pointing from left to right. In S205, such arrows are reserved for different sorts of chemical equation (see, for example, the introduction to Section 6).

Equation 5.1 also has bracketed state symbols after each of the chemical formulae. The four most common such symbols are (s), (l), (g) and (aq), representing solid, liquid, gas and aqueous ion, respectively.

How are we to understand Reaction 5.1? In Section 5.4.1, we saw that the Lewis structure of ammonia (Structure **5.5**) provided each atom with a noble gas shell structure, one non-bonded pair being allocated to nitrogen. In Section 5.4.2 we saw that the Lewis structure of boron trifluoride (Structure **5.11**) left the boron atom two electrons short of a noble gas configuration. If we create an electron-pair bond by allowing the non-bonded electron pair on nitrogen in the ammonia molecule to be shared between the nitrogen and boron atoms, we can write a Lewis structure (Structure **5.14**) in which all atoms, including boron, have a noble gas shell structure. (Note that, in order to focus attention on the bonding electrons, the non-bonded electron pairs on the fluorine atoms have been omitted from Structure 5.14.)

A bond in which the electron pair is provided by just one of the bonded atoms is called a **dative bond**. We need to differentiate such bonds from the more familiar bonds in which *each* bound atom contributes an electron to the electron pair. To do this, we write the dative bonds as arrows running from the 'donor' atom (in this case nitrogen) to the 'receptor' atom (in this case boron). Then Equation 5.1 becomes:

5.14

$$
\begin{array}{ccccc}
\text{H} & & \text{F} & & \text{H}\quad\text{F} \\
| & & | & & |\quad\quad| \\
\text{H}-\text{N} & + & \text{B}-\text{F} & = & \text{H}-\text{N}\longrightarrow\text{B}-\text{F} \\
| & & | & & |\quad\quad| \\
\text{H} & & \text{F} & & \text{H}\quad\text{F}
\end{array}
\qquad (5.2)
$$

Another puzzle solved by the use of dative bonds is the electronic structure of carbon monoxide, CO. If we write the compound C=O, then we get Lewis structure **5.15**, in which oxygen, with two non-bonded pairs, has an octet, but carbon is two electrons short of this noble gas state. Suppose, however, that, in addition, a dative bond is formed by allowing one of the oxygen non-bonded pairs to become shared between oxygen and carbon.

5.15

- Incorporate this in a new structural formula for carbon monoxide.

- See Structure **5.16**; the corresponding Lewis structure is **5.17**. Both oxygen and carbon have octets of electrons, and carbon monoxide has been fitted out with a triple bond. It now conforms to our simple bonding theories rather than violating them.

C≡O

5.16   **5.17**

Dative bonds are also useful when writing Lewis structures for oxoions such as carbonate, CO_3^{2-}. We begin in the usual way (Section 5.4.1) by adding the overall charge to the central atom with highest valency, namely carbon. This means adding two electrons to carbon, which gives the shell structure (2,6). Formation of one C=O double bond and two C→O dative bonds then gives Lewis structure **5.18**, which is equivalent to structural formula **5.19**.

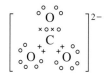

5.18

Before leaving dative bonds, we shall introduce an alternative way of writing them that proves especially useful in organic chemistry. Suppose that atom A forms a dative bond with atom B by donating a non-bonded electron pair to it:

$$A\colon + B = A\colon B \tag{5.3}$$

So far, we have written the dative bond as A→B. But consider atom A before the bond is formed. If we remove one of its lone pair electrons, and put that electron on atom B, we end up with the separate ions $[A^{\bullet}]^{+}$ and $[{\bullet}B]^{-}$. Suppose we now form a conventional shared electron-pair bond from the odd electrons on the two ions. The electrons are shared between the A and B sites in just the way that they are on the right-hand side of Equation 5.3, but the bond would now be written as $\overset{+}{A}-\overset{-}{B}$.

Thus, A→B and $\overset{+}{A}-\overset{-}{B}$ are equivalent ways of writing the dative bond between A and B, and both are equally valid. The structures $H_3N{\rightarrow}BF_3$ and $C{\equiv}O$ can therefore also be written as $H_3\overset{+}{N}-\overset{-}{B}F_3$ and $\overset{-}{C}{\equiv}\overset{+}{O}$.

⬤ Transform Structure **5.19** for the carbonate ion into this new dative bond representation.

⬤ See Structure **5.20**; each C→O bond is replaced by , and $\overset{+}{C}-\overset{-}{O}$ as the carbon atom forms two dative bonds, a charge of +2 must be added to the double negative charge on carbon in Structure **5.19**. This gives zero charge on carbon in the new version, but as there is now a single negative charge on each of the two singly bonded oxygens, the total charge on the ion is −2 as before.

5.4.4 Resonance structures

Gaseous oxygen occurs as O_2 molecules. But ultraviolet light or an electric discharge converts some of the oxygen to ozone (Box 5.4). This has the molecular formula O_3.

A Lewis structure for the O_2 molecule is shown in Figure 5.9a. For ozone too, a Lewis structure can be written which gives each atom a noble gas shell structure (Figure 5.9b); Figures 5.9c and 5.9d give the corresponding structural formulae with alternative representations of the dative bond.

(a)   (b)   (c)   (d)

Figure 5.9 (a) Lewis structure for O_2, each oxygen having the shell structure of neon; (b) Lewis structure for ozone, O_3; (c) and (d) show structural formulae for ozone containing alternative representations of the dative bond.

BOX 5.4 Ozone is blue

Many people know that gaseous ozone in the stratosphere protects us from harmful solar radiation, and that at low altitude it is a source of photochemical smog. But few know that the gas is blue. In the laboratory, ozone is made by exposing O_2 gas to an electric discharge. This yields oxygen containing only 10–15% ozone, and the colour of ozone is then almost imperceptible. But if the gas is passed through a vessel immersed in liquid O_2, it condenses to a liquid mixture of O_2 and ozone; this is cornflower blue. If the liquid is kept cold, a vacuum pump will suck the more volatile O_2 out of it, and the liquid soon separates into two layers. The upper layer is deep blue, and is a 30% solution of ozone in liquid O_2. The lower layer is 30% O_2 in liquid ozone, and has a dark violet colour.

Continued pumping on the lower layer eventually leaves pure liquid ozone, with a deep indigo colour and a boiling temperature of $-112\,°C$ (Figure 5.10). Evaporation normally leads to a violent explosion caused by the decomposition reaction:

$$2O_3(g) = 3O_2(g) \qquad\qquad (5.4)$$

However, clean procedures that exclude dust and organic matter allow slow uninterrupted evaporation. The product is a deep blue gas, which is almost 100% ozone.

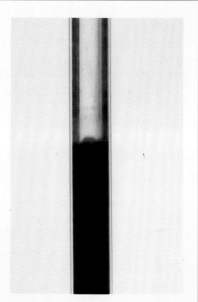

Figure 5.10
The very dark indigo colour of liquid ozone viewed through a cooling bath and the glass of a surrounding vacuum flask.

○ Do Figures 5.9c and d suggest that the lengths of the two bonds in the ozone molecule should be equal or unequal?

○ Unequal; one is a double bond and the other a single dative bond. We would expect this difference to influence their lengths.

But experimental measurement shows that both bonds have the same length (127.8 pm). To account for this, we note that the structures shown in Figures 5.9c and d have companions in which the double and single bonds have simply been exchanged. Figure 5.11, for example, shows Figure 5.9d and its partner. The real structure of the molecule with its equal bond lengths is a sort of average of the two. In situations like this, where a molecule is not adequately represented by a single Lewis structure and seems like a composite of two or more, the competing structures are written down and linked by a double-headed arrow, as shown in Figure 5.11.

The two structures are called **resonance structures**, and the real structure of ozone is said to be a **resonance hybrid** of the two. The significance of the representations in Figure 5.11 is that in ozone, each bond is a mixture of one-half of a double bond and one-half of a single dative bond. Note that Figure 5.11 is not meant to imply that the molecule is constantly changing from one resonance structure to the other. It is a hybrid in the same sense that a mule is a hybrid: it does not oscillate between a horse and a donkey.

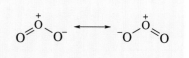

Figure 5.11
The two resonance structures of ozone. The equality of the bond lengths in the real ozone molecule suggests that its actual structure is an average, or superposition of the two.

To clarify this, we turn to benzene, C_6H_6. The reactions of benzene and its derivatives are studied extensively in Book 7. Like ozone, it can be represented as a resonance hybrid of two resonance structures in which all atoms have noble gas configurations (Figure 5.12).

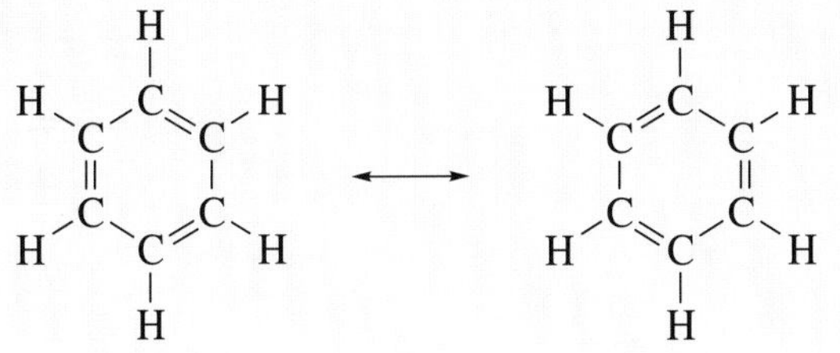

Figure 5.12 The two resonance structures of benzene.

A typical C—C single bond length in an alkane hydrocarbon such as ethane, C_2H_6 (Structure **5.21**), is 154 pm; in contrast, a typical C=C bond length in an alkene hydrocarbon such as ethene, C_2H_4 (Structure **5.22**), is 134 pm. The *individual* resonance structures in Figure 5.12 therefore suggest that the carbon–carbon bond lengths in benzene should alternate between about 134 pm and 154 pm around the ring.

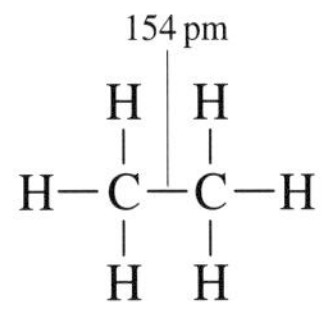

5.21 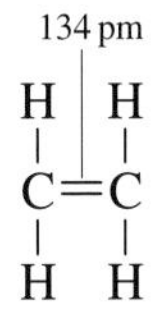   5.22

● But what does the *whole* of Figure 5.12 suggest?

● The real structure of benzene is a hybrid of the individual structures, and each carbon–carbon bond will be a mixture of one-half single and one-half double bonds; all carbon–carbon bond lengths should be equal and lie *between* 134 and 154 pm.

This is precisely the case: all carbon–carbon bond lengths in benzene are 140 pm!

Number the carbon–carbon bonds in a benzene ring of Figure 5.12 clockwise from 1–6. All bonds contain at least one pair of electrons. However, in one of the resonance structures, bonds 1, 3 and 5 are double bonds, each containing a second electron pair; in the other resonance structure, the double bonds and extra pair of electrons are found at bonds 2, 4 and 6. The implication of Figure 5.12 is that in the resonance hybrid these three extra pairs of electrons are not confined to, or *localized* within, just half of the bonds in the ring. Instead, they are **delocalized** around the ring and equally shared within all six bonds. Although, in S205, we shall draw benzene and its derivatives as a single resonance hybrid (Structure **5.23**), remember that this delocalization makes the bond lengths in the ring equal, contrary to the implications of Structure **5.23**.

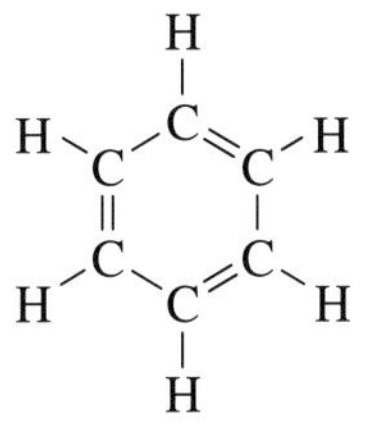

5.23

We conclude with a resonance hybrid which is an ion. Structure **5.20** suggests unequal bond lengths in the carbonate ion. In fact, X-ray crystallography of carbonates suggests that all three bond lengths are equal, at about 129 pm; standard values for C—O and C=O bond lengths are around 143 pm and 120 pm, respectively. Three resonance structures, all equivalent to Structure **5.20** contribute to a resonance hybrid that accounts for the bond length (Figure 5.13).

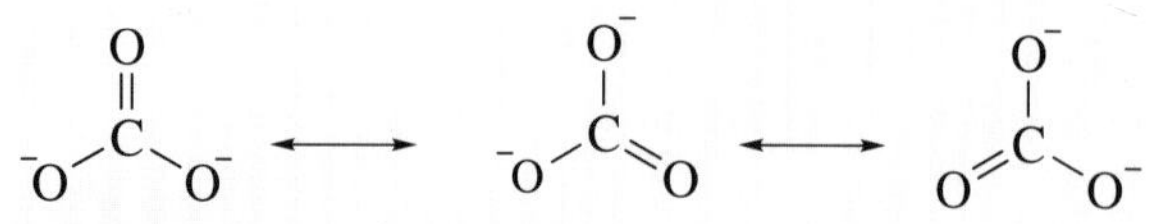

Figure 5.13 The three resonance structures for the carbonate ion. They suggest that all three bonds should be of equal length.

5.5 Summary of Section 5

1   The chemical formulae of many substances can be understood by arguing that their atoms attain noble gas structures by chemical combination.

2   In ionic compounds, this is achieved by the transfer of electrons from one atom to another; in molecular substances, it happens through the sharing of electron pairs in covalent bonds. But in both cases, bonds between atoms consist of shared pairs of electrons. In covalent compounds the sharing is fairly equitable; in ionic compounds it is much less so.

3   In metals, the sharing takes a different form. An 'electron gas' is created by removing electrons from the atoms of the metallic elements. The result is an array of ions steeped in a pool of free electrons. The negatively charged electron gas occupies the space between the ions and pulls them together.

4   Atoms with high but similar electronegativities from the right of Figure 5.5 combine to form covalent substances; those with low but similar electronegativities from the left of Figure 5.5 yield metallic substances. The combination of atoms of low and high electronegativity from the left and right of Figure 5.5 produces ionic compounds.

5   Chemical substances can now be classified, first structurally as either molecular or non-molecular, and second by bond type as ionic, covalent or metallic.

6   In Lewis structures, each covalent bond is represented by a shared electron pair. Double bonds, as in CO_2, require two shared pairs; a triple bond, as in HCN, requires three. These allocations often leave some atoms with non-bonded electron pairs.

7   In many cases, this operation provides each atom with a noble gas shell structure, especially if we introduce dative bonds in which both electrons are contributed by one atom. But in some cases, such as PF_5, it does not.

8   Sometimes the bond lengths in a chemical substance are such that the substance cannot be represented by a single Lewis structure or structural formula. It is better described as a resonance hybrid — an average or superposition of two or more structural formulae called 'resonance structures'.

QUESTION 5.2

Consider the compounds IBr, $CaCl_2$ and $CaMg_2$. One is ionic, one is covalent, and one is metallic. Identify which is which, and match each compound to one of the descriptions below. In each case, suggest whether the compound is molecular or non-molecular.

(i)   White solid that melts at 782 °C. It is a poor conductor of electricity in the solid state, but a good one when melted or dissolved in water.

(ii) Brown–black solid that melts at 41 °C to give a liquid with low electrical conductivity.

(iii) Silvery-looking solid that melts at 720 °C. Whether solid or molten, it is an excellent conductor of electricity.

QUESTION 5.3

Write single Lewis structures, and the corresponding structural formulae, for the following molecules or ions: (a) hypochlorous acid, HOCl; (b) sulfur hexafluoride, SF_6; (c) nitrosyl chloride, ONCl; (d) the amide ion, NH_2^-. In each case, state the number of bonding electron pairs and non-bonded pairs on the atom of highest valency. In which of the four Lewis structures do some atoms not have a noble gas shell structure?

QUESTION 5.4

In the nitrate ion, NO_3^-, the nitrogen atom is central and surrounded by three oxygens. Draw a single Lewis structure for this ion which gives each atom a noble gas shell structure. Also draw two structural formulae for this Lewis structure, each containing a different representation of any dative bonds.

QUESTION 5.5

For the Al_2Br_6 molecule (Figure 2.8), write a single Lewis structure that contains dative bonds and gives each atom a noble gas structure (the bromine atom, like chlorine, has seven electrons in its outer shell). Use the two different representations of the dative bond to draw two structural formulae for the Lewis structure. Experiments on this molecule show that all bond lengths in the Al—Br—Al bridges are identical. Which of your two structural formulae best fits this observation?

QUESTION 5.6

In the nitrate ion, NO_3^-, all three nitrogen–oxygen bonds are of equal length. Is either of the structural formulae in your answer to Question 5.4 consistent with this observation? If not, how do you explain the discrepancy?

MOLECULAR REACTIVITY IS CONCENTRATED AT KEY SITES

6

Reactivity is not spread evenly over a molecule; it tends to be concentrated at particular sites. The consequences of this idea are apparent in the chemistry of many elements. However, in organic chemistry, the idea has proved so valuable that it receives specific recognition through the concept of the **functional group**. Structure **6.1** shows the abbreviated structural formula of hexan-1-ol, an alcohol.

$$CH_3-CH_2-CH_2-CH_2-CH_2-CH_2-OH \quad \textbf{6.1}$$

● Identify the functional group in this molecule.

● It is the fragment $-OH$, which is known as the *alcohol* functional group.

Because reactivity is concentrated at the $-OH$ site, we can, through an informed choice of other chemical reactants, change that site (and sometimes the atoms immediately adjacent to it) into something else *while leaving the rest of the molecule unchanged*. For example, the liquid thionyl chloride, $SOCl_2$, will convert hexan-1-ol into 1-chlorohexane:

$$CH_3CH_2CH_2CH_2CH_2CH_2-OH + SOCl_2 = CH_3CH_2CH_2CH_2CH_2CH_2-Cl + SO_2 + HCl \quad (6.1)$$
hexan-1-ol　　　　　　　　　　　　1-chlorohexane

(Note that in the formulae in this equation we have omitted all the bonds apart from the ones connecting the functional groups to the rest of the molecule; these are known as *condensed structural formulae*.) In this reaction the $-OH$ group has been replaced by $-Cl$. An example of a change in both the functional group and its adjacent atoms is the reaction of hexan-1-ol with chromic acid, H_2CrO_4, which yields hexanoic acid:

$$CH_3CH_2CH_2CH_2CH_2CH_2-OH \xrightarrow{H_2CrO_4} CH_3CH_2CH_2CH_2CH_2-\overset{\displaystyle O}{\overset{\displaystyle \|}{C}}-OH \qquad (6.2)$$
hexanoic acid

Here, the terminal $-CH_2OH$ fragment has been converted into the carboxylic acid functional group, $-COOH$. (Note that an arrow has been used in Equation 6.2. An equals sign — see Box 5.3 — would be inappropriate because the equation is not balanced. This type of equation allows us to concentrate attention on the way in which one molecular fragment, $-CH_2OH$, is transformed into another, $-COOH$. Organic chemists often write equations of this sort, the reagent that brings about the change appearing above the arrow.)

We can divide organic molecules into three parts: the functional groups, their immediate environment, and the rest of the molecule. To a first approximation, we expect a functional group and its immediate environment to respond to a reactant in exactly the same way whatever the rest of the molecule is like. Thus, if we write the many molecules containing an alcohol functional group as $R-OH$, the general form of Reaction 6.1 becomes:

$$R-OH \xrightarrow{SOCl_2} R-Cl \qquad (6.3)$$

Likewise, if we write the many molecules that terminate in the unit $-CH_2OH$ as $R-CH_2OH$, then the general form of Reaction 6.2 becomes:

$$R-CH_2OH \xrightarrow{H_2CrO_4} R-\overset{\displaystyle O}{\underset{\displaystyle ||}{C}}-OH \qquad (6.4)$$

In principle therefore, Reactions 6.3 and 6.4 allow us to predict the response of many very different molecules to thionyl chloride and chromic acid.

To a first approximation, the behaviour of organic functional groups is therefore unaffected by the larger environment of the molecules in which those groups are set. A good example is the reaction of some alcohols with nitric acid, HNO_3 (or $HONO_2$), to give nitrate esters:

$$R-O-H \quad + \quad HONO_2 \longrightarrow R-O-NO_2 \quad + \quad H_2O \qquad (6.5)$$

Thus, hexan-1-ol (Structure **6.1**) yields hexyl nitrate, $CH_3CH_2CH_2CH_2CH_2CH_2-O-NO_2$.

Two organic molecules that contain more than one alcohol functional group are glycerol (Reaction 6.6), made by heating natural fats or oils with sodium hydroxide, and pentaerythritol (Reaction 6.7). Reactions 6.6 and 6.7 show how a mixture of concentrated nitric and sulfuric acid replaces all of the $-OH$ groups with $-O-NO_2$ groups, leaving the rest of the molecules unchanged.

$$\begin{array}{l} CH_2-OH \\ | \\ CH-OH \\ | \\ CH_2-OH \end{array} \xrightarrow{HNO_3/H_2SO_4} \begin{array}{l} CH_2-ONO_2 \\ | \\ CH-ONO_2 \\ | \\ CH_2-ONO_2 \end{array} \qquad (6.6)$$

glycerol $\qquad\qquad\qquad$ nitroglycerine

$$HO-CH_2-\overset{\displaystyle CH_2-OH}{\underset{\displaystyle CH_2-OH}{\overset{\displaystyle |}{\underset{\displaystyle |}{C}}}}-CH_2-OH \xrightarrow{HNO_3/H_2SO_4} O_2NO-CH_2-\overset{\displaystyle CH_2-ONO_2}{\underset{\displaystyle CH_2-ONO_2}{\overset{\displaystyle |}{\underset{\displaystyle |}{C}}}}-CH_2-ONO_2 \qquad (6.7)$$

pentaerythritol $\qquad\qquad\qquad\qquad\qquad$ PETN

Finally, we consider cotton, whose fibres consist of the polymer cellulose. A typical fibre has the formula $[C_6H_7O_2(OH)_3]_n$, where n varies, but may be as large as 2 000. Each $C_6H_7O_2(OH)_3$ unit contains three $-OH$ groups, and at the left of Figure 6.1 two of the units are shown linked together. Figure 6.1 also shows that despite this polymeric situation, all of the $-OH$ groups can still be replaced by $-O-NO_2$ groups through a reaction with mixed nitric and sulfuric acids.

The products of Reactions 6.6, 6.7 and Figure 6.1 are called nitroglycerine, pentaerythritol tetranitrate (PETN) and nitrocellulose, respectively. They are three important high explosives.

What makes functional groups such as $-OH$ so much more reactive than the carbon–hydrogen skeleton to which they are attached? This will be explored in Books 5, 7 and 10, but one comment can be made here. Look again at Structure **6.1** (hexan-1-ol).

Figure 6.1 Cotton is nearly pure cellulose, which is Nature's most common polymer. It is composed of glucose molecules linked through bridging oxygen atoms — a glycosidic linkage (highlighted in red). To the left of the reaction arrow two units are so joined. The six-membered rings are composed of five carbon atoms and one oxygen atom, but here the carbon atom labels have been omitted. Notice the terminal bonds through which the extended chains of the cotton fibre are formed. Replacement of the —OH groups by nitrate groups using a mixture of concentrated nitric and sulfuric acids gives nitrocellulose, a high explosive.

⬤ Which of the 21 atoms in the molecule have non-bonded electron pairs?

⬤ Only one; the oxygen atom of the functional group has two non-bonded electron pairs.

Chemical reactions often occur in steps; in each step, groups of atoms attach themselves to the molecule, undergo change, and then depart. Attractive points of attachment in a molecule will therefore make a reaction more likely.

⬤ Why are non-bonded electron pairs possible points of attachment?

⬤ In Section 5.4.3, you saw that they allow formation of dative bonds.

Such bonds cannot be formed by carbon and hydrogen atoms in hexan-1-ol, because all their outer electrons are used to form strong C—H and C—C bonds. This, then, is one reason why the —OH functional group in **6.1** is the most probable site for a reaction.

Another arises from the fact that functional groups often introduce electronegativity differences into an organic system. For example, the oxygen atom is very electro-negative (Figure 5.5). Thus, in the C—O—H sequence of bonds in any alcohol, the oxygen atom attracts electrons from the adjacent carbon and hydrogen atoms (carbon and hydrogen have similar electronegativities). The oxygen atom of an alcohol therefore carries a fractional negative charge, and the carbon and hydrogen atoms carry fractional positive charges. Any one of the three atoms then becomes a possible point of attachment for the atom of a reagent that carries a fractional charge of opposite sign.

Finally, we remind you of a reservation that we made about functional groups: the idea that their reactions are unaffected by the rest of the molecule is only an approximation. We illustrate the point with another powerful explosive. In phenol, on the left of Reaction 6.8, an —OH group is attached to the benzene ring of Structure **5.23**. Through Reactions 6.5–6.7 and Figure 6.1, we know that the combination HNO_3/H_2SO_4 usually converts an —OH group to a nitrate, —ONO_2, group. But Reaction 6.8 is an exception. The —OH group is untouched, and hydrogen atoms at three points on the benzene ring are replaced by the nitro group, $-NO_2$. The product is a yellow crystalline solid known as 2,4,6-trinitro-phenol or picric acid, whose explosive power exceeds that of TNT (see Box 6.1, pp. 80 and 81). Our expectations about the nitration of $-OH$ functional groups were worked up from cases where the hydrocarbon skeleton is **saturated**; that is, all carbon valencies in the skeleton are used to form *single* bonds to either hydrogen or other carbon atoms. Evidently, the benzene ring, which is not saturated, enhances the reactivity of the hydrogen atoms attached to it, and simultaneously diminishes that of the attached $-OH$ group. The behaviour of a functional group can therefore be affected by its immediate environment. The understanding and deliberate exploitation of such effects is an important part of Books 5, 7 and 10.

$$(6.8)$$

phenol   picric acid

6.1 Summary of Section 6

1   The structural formulae of organic molecules can be divided into the carbon–hydrogen framework or skeleton, and the functional group(s). In the first approximation, the functional groups are the sites where reaction occurs, the framework remaining unreactive.

2   This approximation works best when the framework consists of saturated carbon atoms.

QUESTION 6.1

The compound ethylene glycol (ethane-1,2-diol), $HO-CH_2-CH_2-OH$, is used as antifreeze in car engine coolants. Identify any functional groups in this molecule. Explain how you might make a powerful explosive from ethene glycol, and write down its structural formula.

BOX 6.1 High explosives and propellants

High explosives generate shock waves moving with a velocity of 7 000–9 000 m s^{-1}. Their commercial production began in 1863 when Immanuel Nobel and his son Alfred began manufacturing nitroglycerine at Helenborg near Stockholm (Figure 6.2). Nitroglycerine is a yellow oil prone to accidental explosion, and in 1864, the factory blew up, killing Alfred Nobel's brother Emil. Nevertheless, nitroglycerine proved invaluable in nineteenth century mining engineering projects which required extensive blasting. It was used, for example, to make a way for the Central Pacific railway over the Sierra Nevada, and thus enabled the United States to create the first transcontinental railroad (Figure 6.3). The availability of so dangerous a material in frontier conditions caused many accidents. There are tales of nitroglycerine being mistakenly used in spirit lamps and as a lubricant, things which, as Nobel's biographer laconically remarks, 'were seldom done more than once by the same person'.

Subsequently, Alfred developed the safer dynamites, first by absorbing nitroglycerine with the clay, kieselguhr (guhr dynamite), and then by mixing it with nitrocellulose to form a gel (gelatin dynamite). A mixture of nitrocellulose and nitroglycerine called cordite was the propellant that launched shells from the guns of Royal Navy battleships in both World Wars.

When the hydrocarbons in petrol burn, they acquire the necessary oxygen from the air. High explosives carry their own oxygen, usually in the form of $-NO_2$ groups, which are bound either to oxygen in nitrate esters, or to nitrogen as in RDX (Figure 2.9b), or to carbon as in TNT (Structure **6.2**). In a typical explosion, this oxygen converts the carbon–hydrogen skeleton to steam and oxides of carbon, leaving nitrogen as N_2 molecules. The heat liberated raises the temperature of the products to about 4 000 °C. Thus, for PETN (Reaction 6.7):

$$C(CH_2ONO_2)_4(s) = 2CO(g) + 3CO_2(g) + 4H_2O(g) + 2N_2(g) \qquad (6.9)$$

During the First World War, the principal high explosive used for bursting charges was TNT, supplemented by other substances such as picric acid and ammonium nitrate. In the Second World War, this role was assumed by RDX, supplemented by TNT and PETN. Currently, the chief military explosive is RDX. Semtex, the explosive favoured by terrorists, takes various forms; it usually consists of crystals of RDX embedded in a rubber-like matrix made from a polymer such as polystyrene, or from a wax.

6.2

Figure 6.2
Alfred Nobel (1833–1896) made his fortune through the manufacture of high explosives. In his will, the bulk of his estate was used to fund in perpetuity from 1901 the five Nobel Prizes (for Chemistry, Literature, Peace, Physics, and Physiology or Medicine; a sixth Nobel Prize for Economics was added in 1968), which are awarded annually by Swedish or Norwegian organizations. Nobel appears here at the controls of the equipment that he invented for the manufacture of nitroglycerine. The dangerous nature of the work is revealed by the one-legged stool on which he sits. It protects the operator from the mortal dangers of falling asleep on the job!

Figure 6.3
The creation of the first transcontinental railroad: the Central Pacific, working from the West (left), and the Union Pacific from the East (right) meet at Promontory Point, Utah, where, on 10 May 1869, the 'wedding of the rails' was established with a golden spike driven home with a silver sledgehammer. The Central Pacific outbuilt their rivals by using immigrant Chinese labour and nitroglycerine for blasting.

MOLECULAR SHAPE AFFECTS MOLECULAR REACTIVITY

7

Structural formulae of, for example, hexan-1-ol (Structure **6.1**) and PF$_5$ (Structure **5.13**) merely tell us the immediate neighbours of any particular atom. They are two-dimensional drawings, which ignore the three-dimensional shapes of the molecules. But in studying the structures obtained by X-ray crystallography in Section 2, we recognized that the atoms in a substance have a definite three-dimensional arrangement in space. In other words, molecules have a definite shape and size. Those shapes and sizes are often a key to the understanding of chemical reactions.

Let us start with methane, CH$_4$, and bromomethane, CH$_3$Br. In both molecules, the carbon atoms form four single bonds. It turns out that the four bonds are directed towards the corners of a tetrahedron. The resulting molecular shapes are shown in Figure 7.1 as ball-and-stick representations.

We now take bromomethane (Figure 7.1b) and successively replace each hydrogen atom by a methyl group, CH$_3$, to give the molecules CH$_3$CH$_2$Br, (CH$_3$)$_2$CHBr and (CH$_3$)$_3$CBr. Ball-and-stick representations of each of these molecules are shown at the top of Figure 7.2. At each carbon atom, there are four bonds directed towards the corners of a tetrahedron, and the complexity of the molecular shape therefore increases from left to right, as the number of carbon atoms increases from one to four.

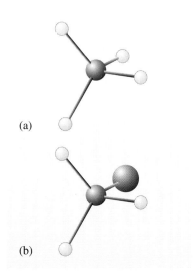

(a)

(b)

Figure 7.1
The structures of (a) methane, CH$_4$; (b) bromomethane, CH$_3$Br.

LEAST CROWDED/MOST REACTIVE   MOST CROWDED/LEAST REACTIVE

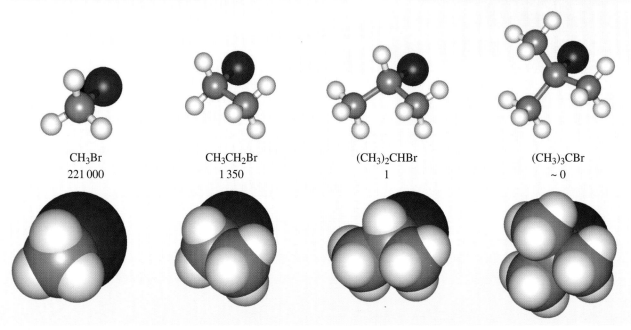

| CH$_3$Br | CH$_3$CH$_2$Br | (CH$_3$)$_2$CHBr | (CH$_3$)$_3$CBr |
| 221 000 | 1 350 | 1 | ~ 0 |

Figure 7.2 The molecules (a) bromomethane, CH$_3$Br; (b) bromoethane, CH$_3$CH$_2$Br; (c) 2-bromopropane, (CH$_3$)$_2$CHBr; (d) 2-bromo-2-methylpropane, (CH$_3$)$_3$CBr, shown in both ball-and-stick (top) and space-filling representations (bottom). Also shown are the relative rates of reaction of the four compounds when they are treated with lithium iodide in acetone (propanone) solution. ⌨

Ball-and-stick representations are a natural three-dimensional development of structural formulae, and they show the disposition of the atoms in space. But by emphasizing the bonds, they fail to reveal the subtleties of the molecular shape created by the different sizes of atoms. In this respect, space-filling models are better. These appear at the bottom of Figure 7.2. In each case, the viewing direction is the same as the ball-and-stick model above. If you wish to examine and manipulate these structures on screen, you can do so in the following Computer Activity.

COMPUTER ACTIVITY 7.1

The instructions for installing and using WebLab ViewerLite are in your Study File. The molecules in Figure 7.2 can be found on the CD-ROM for Book 2 in the *Figures* folder. They have been stored as space-filling models, but can be switched to ball-and-stick, or other forms, as described in the instructions.

Now we shall look at a reaction of these four molecules, all of which contain the same functional group.

○ Identify this functional group.

● It is the bromo group, $-Br$.

So the molecules are of the general type, RBr, where R is the framework to which the functional group is attached. When such bromo compounds are treated with a solution of lithium iodide in the solvent propanone (acetone, Structure **7.1**), they often undergo a reaction in which the bromo group is replaced by an iodo group:

$$RBr + I^- = RI + Br^- \qquad (7.1)$$

What happens in this reaction at the molecular level? As Figure 7.2 shows, the reactant R—Br contains a carbon–bromine bond, C—Br. Bromine is more electronegative than carbon, so the carbon atom in this bond carries a partial positive charge, written $\delta+$, and the bromine atom a partial negative charge, written $\delta-$ (Structure **7.2**). The negatively charged iodide ion will then tend to approach, and become attached to, the positive carbon. As a carbon–iodine bond is formed, the carbon–bromine bond breaks and a bromide ion is ejected. The reaction is therefore a good illustration of an important point made at the end of Section 6: electronegativity differences often contribute to the reactivity of functional groups.

What is interesting, however, is that in this case, the four bromo compounds respond at very different speeds; Figure 7.2 contains their relative rates of reaction with iodide. They decrease from left to right. For example, CH_3Br reacts 221 000 times as quickly as $(CH_3)_2CHBr$, and the reaction of $(CH_3)_3CBr$ is so slow that it appears not to take place at all.

The space-filling molecules explain this. The reaction is one in which an iodide ion must approach and become attached to the carbon atom that is bound to the bromine atom. There is most room for such an approach on the side of the carbon atom that is opposite to the bulky bromine atom — in other words, according to the direction of view depicted in Figure 7.2. Now look at the space-filling models at the bottom of Figure 7.2.

$$H_3C-\overset{\overset{\textstyle O}{\|}}{C}-CH_3$$

7.1

$$\underset{\textstyle 7.2}{\overset{\textstyle \delta+ \quad \delta-}{C-Br}}$$

🔵 Why do you think the reaction with iodide should be easier for CH_3Br than for $(CH_3)_3CBr$?

🔵 In CH_3Br, the carbon atom is very exposed to the incoming iodide. But if hydrogen atoms are replaced by the more bulky methyl groups, this exposure diminishes, until at $(CH_3)_3CBr$ the carbon atom attached to bromine lies at the bottom of a small cavity created by the three surrounding methyl groups. The iodide cannot reach this carbon atom, so no reaction occurs.

The effect that an organic group produces by virtue of its bulk is described as **steric**. Our chosen example is a crude one, but it illustrates an important idea. Whether the reaction occurs or not depends on the ease with which the iodide ion can gain access to the crucial site on the surface of the molecule. Such ideas can be applied to enzymes. Enzymes are protein molecules that facilitate vital biological reactions. They can do this because their molecular surfaces contain *active sites* to which the molecules participating in the reaction (known as *substrates*) can become temporarily bound. The active sites are crevices in the enzyme surface, often of a complicated shape. The substrate has the precise shape required to fit the crevice, but potential competitors that lack this shape are excluded (Figure 7.3). The need for the substrate to bind to the enzyme surface will often weaken other bonds within the substrate itself, encouraging the changes that the enzyme facilitates. So molecular shape has a fundamental role in the chemistry of life. Let us take a more careful look at it.

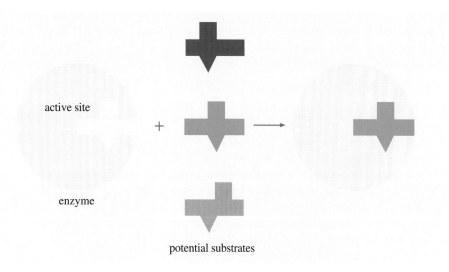

active site

enzyme

potential substrates

Figure 7.3 A model for enzyme action: only one of the three molecules has the shape required to fit the cavity on the enzyme surface; the other two are excluded.

7.1 The shapes of some molecules

Here we shall look at the shapes of some simple molecules of the typical elements. In doing so, we shall meet the problem of representing three-dimensional shapes on two-dimensional paper. Let's use methane, CH_4, as an example. A ball-and-stick representation of this tetrahedral molecule is shown in Figure 7.4. To draw such structures in S205, we shall often make use of the **'flying-wedge notation'**. A flying-wedge representation of the methane molecule of Figure 7.4 is shown in

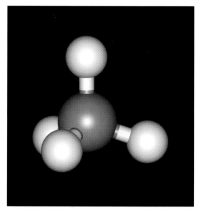

Figure 7.4
A ball-and-stick model of methane, CH_4. 🖥

Figure 7.5. The atom at the pointed or thin end of the wedge is assumed to be in the plane of the paper, and the atom at the thick end is in front of the plane. The connection between this wedge and the perspective of Figure 7.4 is obvious. A continuous line (—) joins two atoms that both lie in the plane of the paper. A dashed line (– –) joins together two atoms, one of which is in the plane of the paper, whereas the other is behind it.

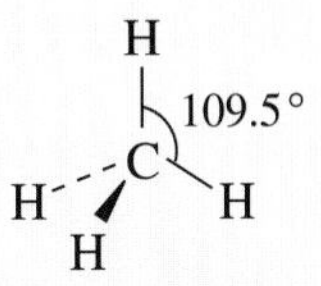

Having established this convention, we shall now examine the shapes of some simple fluorides. In Section 3, we reminded you how to use the Periodic Table to predict the highest fluoride of a typical element.

Figure 7.5
A flying-wedge representation of methane.

⬤ Use Figure 3.3 to predict the highest fluorides of beryllium, boron, carbon, iodine, phosphorus and sulfur.

⬤ The Group numbers are: beryllium, II; boron, III; carbon, IV; phosphorus, V; sulfur, VI; iodine, VII. The predicted highest fluorides are therefore BeF_2, BF_3, CF_4, PF_5, SF_6 and IF_7.

These predictions are correct. All these molecules exist, and their shapes, which have been experimentally determined, are shown in Figure 7.6.

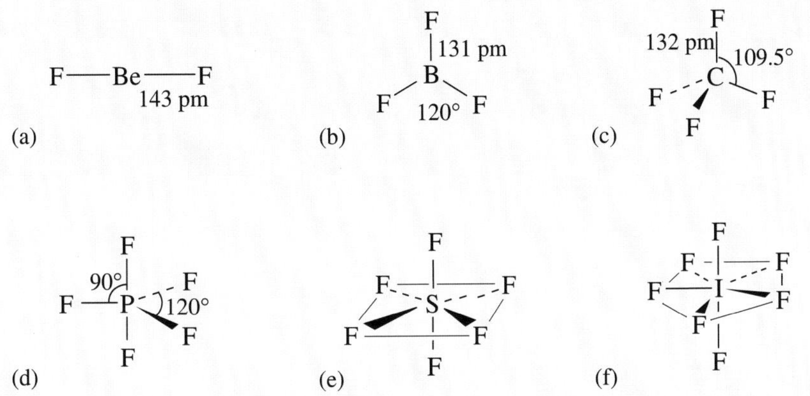

Figure 7.6 The shapes of some fluoride molecules: (a) BeF_2; (b) BF_3; (c) CF_4; (d) PF_5; (e) SF_6; (f) IF_7. They are available in the *Figures* folder on the CD-ROM associated with this Book. 🖳

Beryllium difluoride is a glassy non-molecular solid at room temperature, but the BeF_2 molecule (Figure 7.6a) is obtained when the solid is vaporized by heating it to 1 200 °C. It is linear; that is, the sequence of atoms F—Be—F lies on a straight line. The spatial arrangement of the neighbouring atoms around a particular atom is said to be the **coordination** of that atom. In BeF_2, therefore, the beryllium is in linear coordination.

At 25 °C, BF_3, CF_4, PF_5, SF_6 and IF_7 are all gases containing molecules with the shapes shown in Figure 7.6b–f. In BF_3, all four atoms lie in the same plane, the boron atom forming three B—F bonds to three fluorine atoms at the corners of an equilateral triangle (see Maths Help overleaf). This arrangement of fluorines around boron is called **trigonal planar**. In CF_4, we have the **tetrahedral coordination** around carbon that we have already noted in methane (Figures 7.4 and 7.5).

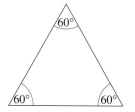

MATHS HELP   EQUILATERAL TRIANGLES

An equilateral triangle (Figure 7.7) has three equal sides, and three internal angles of 60°. The three fluorine atoms in BF_3 lie at the corners of an equilateral triangle. The four faces of a regular tetrahedron, like the one whose corners are defined by the four hydrogen atoms of methane (Figure 7.4), are equilateral triangles. So are the eight faces of a regular octahedron, like the one whose corners are defined by the six chloride ions around each sodium ion in NaCl (Figure 2.10b).

Figure 7.7
An equilateral triangle.

The coordination in PF_5, SF_6 and IF_7 is best described by starting with the horizontal planes containing the central atom of these molecules. In PF_5, this plane contains three P—F bonds directed towards the corners of an equilateral triangle as in BF_3; in SF_6, it contains the sulfur atom with four surrounding fluorines at the corners of a square.

⬤ What does this horizontal plane contain in IF_7?

⬤ The iodine atom, and five I—F bonds directed towards five fluorine atoms at the corners of a regular pentagon.

In all three cases, the coordination is then completed by two other bonds to fluorine at 90° to those in the horizontal plane, one pointing up, and the other pointing down. These arrangments in PF_5, SF_6 and IF_7 are called **trigonal bipyramidal**, **octahedral** and **pentagonal bipyramidal**, respectively.

Figure 7.8
Axial and equatorial positions in PF_5.

In the octahedral molecule SF_6, all the fluorine atoms are equivalent. From each of the fluorine atoms, the view of the rest of the molecule looks the same. But in PF_5 and IF_7, this is not so. There are two kinds of fluorine position: *equatorial positions* in the horizontal plane, and *axial positions* at right-angles to it. In Figure 7.8, these two kinds of position are labelled for the trigonal-bipyramidal arrangement in PF_5.

Why are such arrangements adopted? We can imagine that SF_6 *might* have the shape shown in Structure **7.3**, where the sulfur atom has six S—F bonds directed towards the corners of a regular hexagon, and all seven atoms are in the same plane. But experiment shows the actual shape is the octahedral one shown in Figure 7.6e.

⬤ Suggest a reason for this preference.

⬤ What we are looking for is the idea that the S—F bonds repel one another, so that they get as far apart in space as possible. In Structure **7.3**, they are confined to a single plane and the angle between them is only 60°. By adopting octahedral coordination, the greatest possible separation of the S—F bonds is achieved, the angle being increased to 90°.

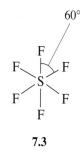

7.3

All the shapes shown in Figure 7.6 conform to this principle by enforcing a good separation of the bonds in space. The principle looks even more reasonable when we remember that we have identified the bonds with pairs of electrons; the like charges of these electron pairs lead to an expectation that one pair will repel another.

However, two very common molecules will soon dispel the notion that repulsion between bonding pairs of electrons is the *sole* determinant of molecular shape. These are water, H_2O, and ammonia, NH_3.

● What would be the shapes of H_2O and NH_3 molecules if they were dictated only by bond–bond repulsions?

● The two O—H bonds of H_2O and the three N—H bonds of NH_3 would get as far apart as possible: H_2O would be linear like BeF_2, and NH_3 would be trigonal planar like BF_3 (see Figure 7.6).

The observed shapes are shown in Structures **7.4** and **7.5**. H_2O is V-shaped and NH_3 is pyramidal. In both cases the inter-bond angle is much closer to the tetrahedral angle of 109.5° than to our predicted values of 180° and 120°, respectively.

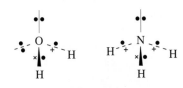

7.4   **7.5**

● What is present in H_2O and NH_3 that might explain these deviations?

● In Section 5.4.1 you saw that the central atoms in these molecules, O and N, carry non-bonded electron pairs. In the molecules of Figure 7.6 this is not the case. If these non-bonded pairs, like the bonding pairs, also exert repulsions, this might explain the unexpected shapes of Structures **7.4** and **7.5**.

Lewis structure **5.6** (p. 68) shows that, around the oxygen atom in water, there are two bonding pairs of electrons and two non-bonded pairs. Structure **5.5** shows that around the nitrogen atom in ammonia, there are three bonding pairs and one non-bonded pair. Thus, both central atoms are surrounded by four pairs of electrons. If these four pairs repel one another, they will be directed towards the corners of a tetrahedron like the four C—F bonds of CF_4 in Figure 7.6c. The resulting arrangements are shown in Figure 7.9. They predict a V-shaped H_2O and a pyramidal NH_3 molecule, with inter-bond angles close to the tetrahedral angle. This agrees with the experimental results indicated in Structures **7.4** and **7.5**. So, if we take account of both bond pairs and non-bonded pairs, can we predict the shapes of molecules of the typical elements?

Figure 7.9
The shapes of the H_2O (left) and NH_3 (right) molecules are consistent with the idea that the four pairs of electrons around the central atoms try to get as far apart as possible. The non-bonded pairs as well as the bonding pairs are involved in this repulsion.

7.2 Valence-shell electron-pair repulsion theory

The theory of molecular shape that we have been working towards is called **valence-shell electron-pair repulsion theory** (VSEPR theory). When applied to molecules and ions of the typical elements, its success rate is high. Here is a stepwise procedure that you can follow when applying this theory. It is illustrated with the molecule XeF_4 and the ion ClO_3^-. Xenon tetrafluoride is one of the select band of noble gas compounds that were unknown before 1962. The chlorate ion, ClO_3^-, is found in potassium chlorate, $KClO_3$, which is a major ingredient of matches. The steps are as follows:

1 Count the number of outer or valence electrons on the central atom.

Our central atoms are xenon and chlorine, for which the numbers of outer electrons are eight and seven, respectively (Figure 4.4).

2 If you are dealing with an ion, add one electron for each negative charge and subtract one electron for each positive charge.

XeF_4 is a neutral molecule, so the number of valence electrons remains eight. The ion ClO_3^- carries a single negative charge, so the number of valence electrons is also eight (7 + 1).

3 Assign these electrons to the bonds.

We assume that the bonds formed by the central atom with the halogens or hydrogen are single bonds consisting of one electron pair. Each atom of the bond contributes one electron to this pair. In XeF_4, xenon forms four such bonds, so four of its eight outer electrons are used in this way.

At first sight, bonds formed to oxygen are more complicated. Oxygen has six outer electrons, and it can complete its octet in two ways. Both ways are apparent in the structure for ozone (Figure 5.9c and d). One of the terminal oxygen atoms forms a double bond with the central atom; this bond consists of two shared electron pairs. The other terminal oxygen atom receives a pair of electrons from the central atom, which is the donor in a dative bond. *But in both types of bond, the central atom contributes two electrons.* Now in ClO_3^- the central chlorine forms three bonds to oxygens. Six of its eight electrons are therefore used in these bonds.

4 Divide any outer electrons not used in bonding into non-bonded pairs as far as possible.

In XeF_4, subtraction of the four xenon bonding electrons from the total of eight leaves four electrons or two non-bonded pairs. In ClO_3^-, subtraction of the six bonding chlorine electrons from the total of eight leaves one non-bonded pair. Each bond, and each non-bonded pair, is now regarded as a **repulsion axis**, an axis of negative charge that repels other such axes.

5 Count each non-bonded pair and each bond as a repulsion axis. Select the appropriate disposition of these repulsion axes from Figure 7.6.

The theory assumes that the repulsion axes mimic the bonds formed with fluorine in Figure 7.6 by getting as far apart as possible. For XeF_4, four bonds and two non-bonded pairs give six repulsion axes, and Figure 7.6 tells us that these will have an octahedral disposition. For ClO_3^-, three bonds and one non-bonded pair give four repulsion axes with a tetrahedral disposition.

6 Choose between any alternative arrangements by minimizing inter-axis repulsion.

In many cases, the shape is fully determined at the end of step 5. This is the case for ClO_3^-. We have predicted the shape shown in Structure **7.6**, and this suggests that ClO_3^- should be pyramidal with an inter-bond angle close to the tetrahedral angle of 109.5°. The experimentally observed value is 105°.

In some cases, however, a choice between two or more possibilities must be made. XeF_4 is one of these. The two non-bonded pairs and four bonds can be octahedrally disposed in two ways (Structures **7.7** and **7.8**). It can be quite difficult to choose

7.6

7.7

7.8

between such competing arrangements, but a useful procedure assumes that the inter-axis repulsions vary as follows:

non-bonded pair–non-bonded pair > non-bonded pair–bond pair > bond pair–bond pair

The shape can then usually be obtained by choosing that possibility in which the strongest of these different repulsions is minimized. In the case of XeF_4, the strongest repulsion is of the non-bonded pair–non-bonded pair type.

⬤ Is this type of repulsion lower in Structure **7.7** or Structure **7.8**?

⬤ In Structure **7.8**, where the angle between the non-bonded pairs is 180°, so they are as far apart as possible.

This suggests that XeF_4 is planar in shape, the xenon atom being surrounded by four fluorines at the corners of a square (hence the shape is referred to as **square planar**). Experimentally this is found to be the case.

7.2.1 Refinements and difficulties

In Section 7.2, we said that inter-axis repulsions vary in the order:

non-bonded pair–non-bonded pair > non-bonded pair–bond pair > bond pair–bond pair

There is evidence for this in the inter-bond angles in molecules. For example, in water and ammonia (Structures **7.4** and **7.5**), the bond angles are about 5° and 2° less than the tetrahedral angle of 109.5°.

⬤ Does this support the quoted order of inter-axis repulsions?

⬤ Yes; non-bonded pair–bond pair repulsions tend to reduce the inter-bond angle; bond pair–bond pair repulsions tend to increase it. The observed reduction shows that non-bonded pair–bond pair repulsions are dominant. The reduction is greater in H_2O than NH_3 because the water molecule has two non-bonded pairs.

Similar effects suggest that there are differences in the repulsive effects of single, double and triple bonds. As Lewis theory implies that these consist of one, two and three pairs of electrons, we might expect that their repulsive effects would vary in the order: triple bond > double bond > single bond. The geometry of the ethene molecule can be seen in Structure **7.9**. The four outer electrons on each carbon atom are distributed between three repulsion axes: one double bond to carbon and two single bonds to hydrogen.

7.9

⬤ Do the inter-bond angles support our assumed difference in the repulsive effects of single and double bonds?

⬤ Yes; the stronger repulsion exerted by the C=C bond forces the two C—H bonds together. The inter-bond angle falls below 120°, the value for regular trigonal-planar coordination.

Recognition of the different repulsive effects of single and double bonds can therefore be useful in choosing a molecular shape or predicting bond angles.

Nevertheless, when step 5 of the procedure of Section 7.2 leaves us with two or more structures to choose from, it is sometimes hard to make an informed choice. Minimizing the strongest repulsions is usually effective, but not always. A particular problem can arise when there are five repulsion axes — the trigonal-bipyramidal disposition. We can illustrate it with ClF_3, a liquid that boils at 12 °C, and reacts with water with a sound like the crack of a whip. The central chlorine atom has seven outer electrons, three of which are used in forming the three Cl—F bonds. The other four electrons become two non-bonded pairs, which, with the three bonds, give us five repulsion axes disposed in the trigonal-bipyramidal arrangement. There are three possibilities (Structures **7.10**–**7.12**):

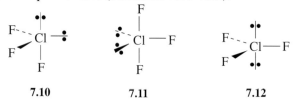

| 7.10 | 7.11 | 7.12 |

In all three, the strongest repulsive interaction is of the non-bonded pair–non-bonded pair type. If we minimize this, we would decisively reject **7.10**, where the non-bonded pair axes are at right-angles, and choose **7.12**, where they both occupy the axial positions and so are at 180° to one another. This predicts a planar ClF_3 molecule. But experiment shows that the correct structure is **7.11**, where the non-bonded pairs occupy equatorial positions at 120° to each other. Indeed, it seems that in molecules based on the trigonal-bipyramidal disposition of repulsion axes, the non-bonded pairs avoid the axial, and occupy the equatorial sites. In this case, our recommended procedure must be modified.

Note that throughout this Section we have confined ourselves to typical element molecules containing an even number of valence electrons. The valence electrons can then always be divided into pairs, and each repulsion axis consists of a pair or pairs of electrons. But a few typical element molecules contain an odd number of electrons, and the application of VSEPR theory then forces us to deal with repulsion axes consisting of a single electron. An example of this sort is considered in Question 7.6 below.

Finally, you should recognize that the restriction of VSEPR theory to typical elements is important. It is very much less successful in predicting the molecular shape of transition-metal compounds.

7.3 Summary of Section 7

1   Molecules have a three-dimensional shape. Bulky irregularities in the shape of a molecule around a reactive site can exclude a potential reactant. Such effects are described as steric.

2   A sufficient refinement of the molecular shape in the region of the reactive site can make that site specific to just one particular reactant. Many enzymes operate in this way.

3   The shapes of simple molecules can be predicted using valence-shell electron-pair repulsion theory. The valence electrons of a central atom are divided between the bonds to other atoms, and non-bonded pairs, each bond or non-bonded pair constituting a repulsion axis. The total number of repulsion axes

determines their arrangement in space (see Figure 7.6): two, linear; three, trigonal planar; four, tetrahedral; five, trigonal bipyramidal; six, octahedral; seven, pentagonal bipyramidal.

4 A choice between alternative distributions of bonds and non-bonded pairs within any one of these arrangements can usually be made by minimizing the strongest types of repulsion. In making this choice, the following points are relevant:

(i) Repulsive effects involving non-bonded pairs and bond pairs vary in the order:

non-bonded pair–non-bonded pair > non-bonded pair–bond pair > bond pair–bond pair

(ii) Multiple bonds exert stronger repulsions than single bonds.

(iii) In a trigonal-bipyramidal distribution of repulsion axes, non-bonded pairs occupy equatorial rather than axial positions.

QUESTION 7.1

The six carbon atoms of benzene, C_6H_6, lie at the corners of a regular hexagon, and each one carries a hydrogen atom. In compounds **7.13–7.16** below, some of these hydrogen atoms have been replaced by other groups. In each case, a carboxylic acid functional group, $-COOH$, is present.

7.13	7.14	7.15	7.16

The $-COOH$ group is normally converted to $-COOCH_3$ when a compound containing it is heated in a solution containing hydrogen chloride and methanol, CH_3OH. When compounds **7.13–7.16** are subjected to this treatment, **7.13** and **7.16** react as expected, forming $C_6H_5COOCH_3$ and $(CH_3)_3C_6H_2CH_2COOCH_3$, respectively. But compounds **7.14** and **7.15** undergo little or no reaction. Explain these differences.

QUESTION 7.2

By heating the solids $BeCl_2$ and $SnCl_2$ to quite moderate temperatures, discrete gaseous $BeCl_2$ and $SnCl_2$ molecules can be obtained. What shapes and bond angles would you expect the molecules to have?

QUESTION 7.3

Predict the shapes of the ions (i) NH_4^+; (ii) ICl_2^- (central atom I); (iii) PCl_6^- (central atom P).

QUESTION 7.4

Predict the shapes and bond angles in the molecules (i) BrF_5 (central atom Br) and (ii) SF_4 (central atom S).

QUESTION 7.5

Predict the shape and bond angle of (i) the sulfur dioxide molecule, SO_2 (central atom S), and (ii) the shape of the molecule $XeOF_4$ (central atom Xe).

QUESTION 7.6

For a compound of the typical elements, the brown gas nitrogen dioxide, NO_2, is unusual in that its molecule contains an odd number of electrons. Consequently, when applying VSEPR theory to it, a repulsion axis consisting of a single electron is the result. Use VSEPR theory to predict the shape and likely bond angle of NO_2 by assessing the repulsive effect that this single-electron repulsion axis might have.

REACTIVITY NEEDS A FAVOURABLE RATE AND EQUILIBRIUM CONSTANT

8

So far, we have concentrated on the electronic and spatial structures of chemical substances, but we have not said much about chemical reactions. Now we turn to the question of why chemical reactions happen. To remind you of the basic ideas, we shall concentrate on one particular reaction which occurs in the modern motor car.

Table 8.1 shows typical percentages of the main constituents of the exhaust gas that emerges from a modern car engine. The two most dangerous pollutants are carbon monoxide, CO, and nitric oxide (strictly known as *nitrogen monoxide*), NO. Both are very poisonous gases. For example, when nitric oxide emerges from the exhaust into the open air and cools down, it reacts with oxygen to form nitrogen dioxide, NO_2 (Figure 8.1). This causes respiratory problems even at very low concentrations, and features in the 'air watch' bulletins given in regional weather forecasts.

Table 8.1

The percentage by volume of the different gases in a typical car exhaust stream

Gas	Volume per cent
nitrogen and argon	71.0
carbon dioxide	13.5
water vapour	12.5
carbon monoxide	0.68
oxygen	0.51
hydrogen	0.23
nitric oxide	0.11
hydrocarbons	0.05

Figure 8.1 Brown nitrogen dioxide gas being produced, in this case, by the reaction of copper with concentrated nitric acid.

Given these dangers, there is a reaction that could be very beneficial:

$$2NO(g) + 2CO(g) = N_2(g) + 2CO_2(g) \qquad (8.1)$$

If NO and CO reacted like this, then the nitric oxide in the exhaust would disappear, and take a substantial amount of poisonous carbon monoxide with it. Unfortunately, the reaction does not seem to happen. Why is this?

8.1 Is the equilibrium position unfavourable?

The first possibility is that the reaction system has been able to reach chemical equilibrium, but the equilibrium position is not favourable. How does this come about? If equilibrium has been reached, then the forward (left to right) and backward (right to left) reactions are occurring at equal rates. In such a case, we can emphasize the fact by writing the reaction with two opposed, half-headed arrows:

$$2NO(g) + 2CO(g) \rightleftharpoons N_2(g) + 2CO_2(g) \qquad (8.2)$$

This indicates that both the forward reaction:

$$2NO(g) + 2CO(g) \longrightarrow N_2(g) + 2CO_2(g) \tag{8.3}$$

and the backward reaction:

$$N_2(g) + 2CO_2(g) \longrightarrow 2NO(g) + 2CO(g) \tag{8.4}$$

are taking place: at the microscopic, molecular level there is ceaseless change in both directions. However, at equilibrium, *the overall rates of the forward and backward reactions are equal*. The reaction system then *seems* static because, at the macroscopic level where we measure things, there is no apparent change in the amounts or concentrations of any of the four gases involved. Suppose that Reaction 8.1 appears not to occur because, although it has reached equilibrium, the equilibrium position is unfavourable. Then it must be that the rates of the forward and backward reactions become equal when the concentrations of the reactants (NO and CO) are very high, and those of the products (N_2 and CO_2) are very small, so small as to be undetectable. This possibility can be tested by examining the *equilibrium constant*, K, for the reaction.

8.1.1 The equilibrium constant

An expression for the equilibrium constant of a reaction can be put together from the concentrations of the reactants and products at equilibrium. A concentration of a reactant or product is represented by enclosing its chemical formula in square brackets. Thus, the concentration of NO(g) is written [NO(g)].

To write down the equilibrium constant of a reaction, we start with the concentrations of the products. Each one is raised to the power of the number that precedes it in the reaction equation, and the corresponding terms for each product are then multiplied together.

- Do this now for the products of the equilibrium system 8.2.

- The result is $[N_2(g)] \times [CO_2(g)]^2$, or, taking the multiplication sign as understood, $[N_2(g)][CO_2(g)]^2$. In Equation 8.2, $CO_2(g)$ is preceded by a two, so its concentration is squared.

- Now repeat the operation for the reactants in Equation 8.2.

- The result is $[NO(g)]^2[CO(g)]^2$; in Equation 8.2, both NO(g) and CO(g) are preceded by a two.

The equilibrium constant, K, is obtained by dividing the result for the products by the result for the reactants:

$$K = \frac{[N_2(g)][CO_2(g)]^2}{[NO(g)]^2[CO(g)]^2} \tag{8.5}$$

We have raised the possibility that Reaction 8.1 does not happen because the equilibrium position for equilibrium system 8.2 lies well over to the left. In other words, at equilibrium, the concentrations of NO(g) and CO(g) are very high, and those of $N_2(g)$ and $CO_2(g)$ are so small as to be undetectable.

● If so, will K be large or small?

● It will be very small because the large quantities ([NO(g)] and [CO(g)]) occur on the bottom of Equation 8.5, and the small quantities ([N_2(g)] and [CO_2(g)]) occur on the top.

The value of K can be determined experimentally. A typical temperature in a car exhaust system is 525 °C. At this temperature, K turns out to be 10^{40} mol^{-1} litre.

● Given this information, does the equilibrium position lie to the left of Equation 8.2?

● No; K is immense, so at equilibrium, the concentrations of the products (which appear on top of the fraction in Equation 8.5) must be much greater than those of the reactants (which appear on the bottom). The equilibrium position for Reaction 8.2 at 525 °C therefore lies well over to the right.

8.2 Is the rate of reaction very slow?

If the equilibrium position is very favourable, then the reason why Reaction 8.1 fails to occur at 525 °C must be that its rate is very slow. Usually, a reasonable response would be to increase the temperature yet further, but the structure and economy of the car gives us little scope to do this. The alternative is to use a **catalyst**, which leaves the equilibrium constant unchanged, while speeding the reaction up.

Let us look at the changes that take place in the internal energy as reactants change progressively into products. Figure 8.2 shows a simplified version. The internal energies of the reactants (2NO + 2CO) and products (N_2 + 2CO_2) are marked by two 'platforms'. The platform for the products lies lower than that for the reactants. This shows that the internal energy change during the reaction is negative.

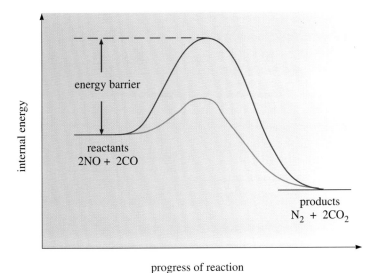

progress of reaction

Figure 8.2 A simplified version of the change that takes place in the internal energy of the molecules as nitric oxide and carbon monoxide change into nitrogen and carbon dioxide. The upper (red) curve shows the change in the absence of a catalyst; the lower (blue) curve, the change when a catalyst is present.

Between the reactants and products, the internal energy does not decrease gradually as the reaction progresses; instead, it rises initially, reaches a maximum, and then declines. The upper curve shows the situation in the absence of a catalyst. The internal energy of the reacting molecules must first increase by an amount marked 'energy barrier' in Figure 8.2.

● How might the reactants, NO and CO, acquire this extra energy?

● One possible source is the kinetic energy of other molecules. Lucky collisions may provide some NO and CO molecules with unusually high energies. If these high-energy molecules then chance to collide with each other, they might be able to surmount the energy barrier and react with each other.

This also explains why an increase in temperature increases the rate of a reaction: a temperature rise increases the speed of the molecules, and the required increase in internal energy following collisions then becomes more probable. But as we have seen, in this case the rate is not great even at 525 °C. The energy barrier must be high. The main reason is a property of nitric oxide. In Reaction 8.1, the nitrogen and oxygen atoms in NO must be separated at some point, but the bond that holds them together is very strong. A large input of energy is therefore needed to bring the separation about, so the energy barrier is high and the reaction is slow.

BOX 8.1 The three-way catalytic converter

The solution to the high energy barrier for Reaction 8.1 is to involve a third party — a catalyst. A suitable material is the metal rhodium. When NO and CO molecules enter a catalytic converter, they become bound to rhodium surfaces. The binding of NO to rhodium weakens the bond between the N and O atoms, and the NO unit becomes more vulnerable to change. For example, it is believed that in some cases, the bond is so weakened that the N and O atoms separate completely, and move about on the rhodium surface. Pairs of nitrogen atoms can then meet, combine and leave the surface as $N_2(g)$; oxygen atoms can meet and combine with CO molecules on the surface, leaving as $CO_2(g)$.

Obviously, this type of reaction pathway is very different from one that takes place entirely in the gas phase with no catalyst present. Most particularly, because the catalyst surface assists the breaking of the bond in the NO molecule, it has a lower energy barrier (see Figure 8.2) and is much faster. In a *three-way catalytic converter*, some 90% of the nitric oxide in the exhaust stream is converted to nitrogen and carbon dioxide. Figure 8.3 shows an example. The catalyst actually contains rhodium and platinum. The platinum catalyses the reactions of both carbon monoxide and unburnt hydrocarbons (from the petrol) with oxygen, giving carbon dioxide and steam. The converter is called 'three way' because it thereby removes all three main types of pollutant: nitrogen oxides, carbon monoxide and unburnt hydrocarbons. Figure 8.4 provides you with further details.

Figure 8.3
A three-way catalytic converter; the metal shell has been partially cut away, exposing a gauze lining, inside which is the cylindrical grid of exhaust channels. A separate grid of this type is shown above and to the left. It is black because the platinum–rhodium catalyst has been dispersed over its surfaces. Before the catalyst is spread over it, the ceramic grid is white, as shown above and to the right.

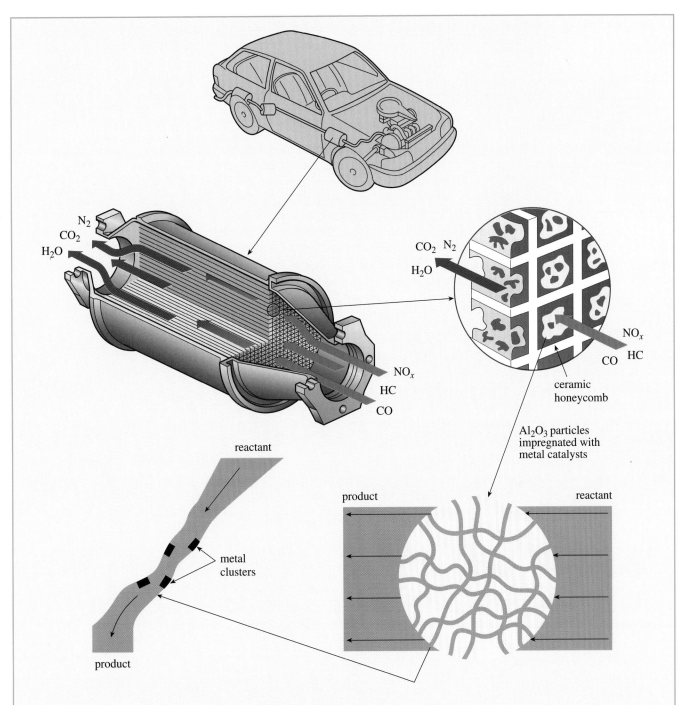

Figure 8.4 The core of a typical three-way catalytic converter consists of a cylindrical grid of thin-walled channels of square cross-section, composed of a ceramic material made from oxides of magnesium, aluminium and silicon. The platinum–rhodium catalyst is dispersed over granules of solid aluminium oxide, Al_2O_3, which have been specially prepared with a high surface area. The catalyst-coated granules are mixed with water to form a slurry, and passed through the grid, which is then heated in a furnace. The process leaves Al_2O_3, impregnated with catalyst particles, dispersed on the walls of the channels. In passing through the channels, exhaust pollutants traverse pores in the Al_2O_3 granules, encountering metal catalyst sites where reactions such as that shown in Equation 8.1 occur. Efficient conversion occurs only if the air–fuel ratio on entry to the converter is right. The ratio is controlled mainly by measuring the oxygen with a sensor and then making any necessary adjustments to the air and fuel supply (NO_x denotes oxides of nitrogen; HC denotes hydrocarbons).

8.3 Equilibrium positions and rates of reaction in S205

Section 8 showed that if a reaction is to occur at a particular temperature, two conditions must be fulfilled: its equilibrium constant must be sufficiently large, and its rate sufficiently great. We finish by pointing out how this crucial distinction between the equilibrium constant and the rate reveals itself in Figure 8.2. The figure shows two different pathways by which the reactants can change into the products, but both routes begin at the *same* reactant energy level, and finish at the *same* product energy level. Regardless of reaction pathway, the energy difference between reactants and products is the same. As you will see in Book 4, it is an energy difference between reactants and products that determines the equilibrium constant of a reaction, and therefore the equilibrium position. The fact that both pathways have the same energy difference, and therefore the same equilibrium constant, shows that the equilibrium constant in a reaction is quite unaffected by *how* reactants change into products. With equilibrium constants, the nature and energies of the initial and final states are everything; what happens in between is immaterial.

After Book 4, the emphasis shifts to the rate of reaction. Here, the reaction pathway is crucial. In Figure 8.2, both routes start with the same reactants, and end with the same products, but the intervening stages along each pathway are very different. Such sequences of intervening stages are called **reaction mechanisms**, and the mechanism in the presence of a catalyst delivers a smaller energy barrier and a faster rate than the one that pertains when the catalyst is absent. With rates of reaction, therefore, the mechanism is crucial. In Book 5, we shall look at rates and reaction mechanisms in detail.

8.4 Summary of Section 8

1   The equilibrium constant of a reaction is fixed at any particular temperature. It depends only on the natures of the initial reactants and the final products; what happens as reactants change into products has no effect on the equilibrium constant or position of equilibrium.

2   The rate of a chemical reaction is affected both by the temperature and by the pathway (reaction mechanism) through which reactants change into products. This pathway can sometimes be altered, for example by the introduction of a catalyst.

3   The catalyst causes a change in the reaction mechanism which leads to a lowering of the energy barrier and to a greater rate of reaction.

QUESTION 8.1

The combination of sulfur dioxide with oxygen, and the decomposition of steam into hydrogen and oxygen are both reactions of great potential practical value. These reactions, and their equilibrium constants at 427 °C (700 K) are as follows:

$$2SO_2(g) + O_2(g) = 2SO_3(g); \qquad\qquad K = 10^6 \, mol^{-1} \, litre$$
$$2H_2O(g) = 2H_2(g) + O_2(g); \qquad\qquad K = 10^{-33} \, mol \, litre^{-1}$$

Write down expressions for the equilibrium constants of the two reactions. When the two reactions are attempted at 700 K, neither seems to occur. Which of the two might be persuaded to occur at this temperature, and what form might your 'persuasion' take?

REVIEWING AND REFLECTING ON BOOK 2

9

Figure 9.1 is a conceptual diagram that summarizes Book 2. The title of S205 is *The Molecular World*, but molecules are made of atoms, so it was with atoms, to the left of Figure 9.1, that we began. Early in Section 2 they acquired a structure with a positively charged nucleus surrounded by negatively charged electrons. To a chemist, the most important property of an *atom* is the number of positive charges in its nucleus. This *atomic number* distinguishes one chemical element from another: atoms with the same atomic number are atoms of the same chemical element. This is true even when those atoms have different numbers of *neutrons* in their nuclei. They are then said to be *isotopes* of the same chemical element.

Having labelled atoms with a chemical symbol for the elements that they represent, we then looked, in the rest of Section 2, at how atoms combine with each other. Combination can occur with other atoms of the same element; this yields the elements that are familiar to us as chemical substances. Alternatively, combination can occur between atoms of different elements when a chemical compound is produced. In both cases, it proved useful to look at the distribution of the atoms in space. This led to a classification of chemical substances into *molecular* and *non-molecular* types. Molecular substances contained discrete molecular units well separated from other units of the same formula. For non-molecular substances, this separation could not be made. The distinction is elaborated in the first half of Book 3, which draws most of its examples from the solid state.

In Section 3, atomic number was exploited again: when the chemical elements are laid out in order of atomic number, elements with similar properties appear at regular intervals. This *chemical periodicity* is represented by Periodic Tables, which reveal many regularities in chemical properties. S205 is concerned especially with the typical elements, and therefore with the mini-Periodic Table containing just this sub-set. To explain chemical periodicity, we looked at the arrangement of the negatively charged *electrons* around the positively charged nuclei of the different elements. This was done in Section 4. The *electronic structures* of the ground states of atoms were represented both by electronic configurations, which allocate electrons to sub-shells, and by box diagrams, which also show the spin of the electrons and the number of atomic orbitals within each sub-shell. It transpires that atoms in the same group of the Periodic Table have similar outer electronic configurations, and this points to explanations of chemical properties that depend on electronic structure. Such properties feature particularly in Book 9.

These explanations require an understanding of the chemical bonding through which the atoms of an element express their valencies. In Section 5, we revisited the simplest theories of chemical bonding, which involve the sharing of electron pairs. This sharing, whose nature depends on the electronegativities of the elements, can result in *ionic, covalent or metallic bonding*. Structure from Section 2, and bonding from Section 5, then combined to provide a classification of chemical substances in general: they are molecular covalent, non-molecular ionic, non-molecular covalent or non-molecular metallic. Many compounds of the typical elements, including nearly all organic compounds, are of the molecular covalent type. In S205 therefore,

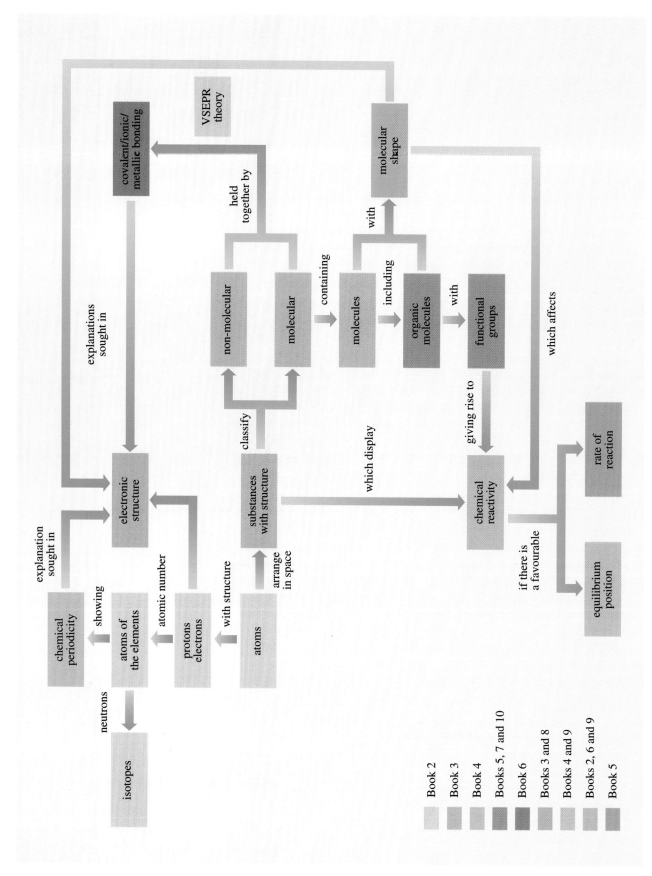

Figure 9.1 A conceptual diagram showing the important ideas in Book 2 and the relationship between them. The diagram is colour-coded to show the S205 Blocks where these ideas are extended and developed.

spectroscopic techniques which provide information about the shapes and structures of molecules in such substances will be especially important. These are the subject of Book 8.

S205, therefore, contains much non-metal and organic chemistry in which covalent bonding is the prevailing bond type. So the rest of Section 5 modified and extended the ideas of shared electron pair bonds. The shared pair can sometimes come from just one of the two atoms in the bond, which is then said to be dative. For many typical element compounds, it is possible to claim both electron-pair bonds and the attainment of a noble gas configuration for the constituent atoms. In some compounds, such as benzene and ozone, the bond lengths call for a representation that is an average of two or more Lewis structures, rather than just one. This phenomenon is called 'resonance'. This part of Section 5 was a piecemeal attempt to patch up elementary bonding theories initiated in particular by the work of G. N. Lewis. It signals the need for a fresh look at the whole subject of chemical bonding. This will be done in Book 6.

From chemical bonding, we turned, in Section 6, to chemical reactions at the molecular level. Some parts of a molecule are more vulnerable to attack by a particular reactant than others, a point well illustrated by the *functional groups* of *organic molecules*. The reactions of functional groups, however, are not entirely independent of their immediate molecular environment. The shapes of organic molecules, which are explored in Book 3 Part 2, also influence them. In Section 7, we pointed to the important steric influences of *molecular shape*, which reach a very sophisticated degree of development in the workings of enzymes. This subject — the functional groups of organic molecules, and the way in which their reactions are affected by molecular shape and electronic structure — is a dominant theme in Books 5, 7 and 10. Although the three-dimensional distribution of the atoms within substances was a part of Sections 2 and 5, this explicit recognition of its importance calls for a theory of molecular shape. For the typical elements this is provided by valence-shell electron-pair repulsion theory (*VSEPR theory*), in which the molecular shape is dictated by repulsions between bonding and non-bonding pairs of valence electrons.

Our growing emphasis on chemical reactivity at the expense of structure and bonding became paramount in Section 8, where the question of why chemical reactions happen was analysed in terms of *equilibrium positions* and *rates of reaction*. In a closed system, a reaction with a tiny equilibrium constant cannot happen under any circumstances; but if a reaction that does not occur is found to have a large equilibrium constant, then the failure to react must be caused only by a slow rate; this can sometimes be increased by the use of a catalyst. Fuller development of this crucial distinction is an important part of S205. The aspect of equilibrium position is taken forward in Book 4, using the reactions of metals as examples; the rate aspect is the subject of Book 5, where examples are drawn mainly, but not exclusively, from organic chemistry.

LEARNING OUTCOMES

1   Recognize valid definitions of, and use in a correct context, the terms, concepts and principles in the following Table. (All Questions)

List of scientific terms, concepts and principles introduced in Book 2

Term	Page number	Term	Page number
allotrope	44	molecular formula	41
alloy	66	non-bonded electron pair	68
atomic number	36	normal oxide	51
atomic orbital	58	octahedral coordination	86
bond pair	68	parallel spins	60
box diagram	60	pentagonal bipyramidal coordination	86
catalyst	95		
chemical element	36	reaction mechanism	98
coordination	85	repulsion axis	88
dative bond	70	resonance hybrid	72
delocalized electrons	73	resonance structure	72
electron gas	65	saturated hydrocarbon	79
electron spin	58	spin	58
empirical formula	40	square-planar coordination	89
extended structure	43	steric effect	84
flying-wedge notation	84	structural formula	66
functional group	76	tetrahedral coordination	85
ground state	60	trigonal-bipyramidal coordination	86
Hund's rule	60	trigonal-planar coordination	85
Lewis structure	63	valence-shell electron-pair repulsion theory (VSEPR)	87
lone pair (of electrons)	68		

2　Explain the connection between the atomic number, the mass number and the number of neutrons in the nucleus for any particular isotope. (Question 2.1)

3　Explain the distinction between the concepts of empirical and molecular formula with reference to chemical compounds. (Question 2.2)

4　Distinguish molecular and non-molecular compounds by using information on their structural and physical properties. (Question 2.3)

5　Identify typical elements from particular properties by using the appropriate section of the Periodic Table, and predict unknown properties of named elements. (Question 3.1)

6　Relate the Group and Period numbers of a typical element in the Periodic Table to its outer electronic configuration, and to the probable formula of its highest fluoride and normal oxide. (Questions 4.1–4.3)

7　Write down the electronic configuration of the free atom of a typical element, either as a string of occupied sub-shells, or as a box diagram. (Questions 4.1–4.4)

8　Given a Periodic Table and/or a knowledge of the electronegativity trends within it, make an assessment of whether a given element or binary compound is likely to be ionic, covalent or metallic. (Question 5.2)

9　Represent discrete molecules or simple polyatomic ions of the typical elements as either structural formulae or Lewis structures. (Questions 5.1 and 5.3–5.6)

10　Draw resonance structures, given the molecular geometry and bond length data for highly symmetrical molecules. (Questions 5.5 and 5.6)

11　Use the functional groups in an organic molecule to predict some of the possible reactions that the compound might undergo. (Question 6.1)

12　Given the shape of an organic molecule, use a rough assessment of the relative sizes of its component groups to predict possible steric effects on its reactivity. (Question 7.1)

13　Use valence-shell electron-pair repulsion (VSEPR) theory to predict the shapes of simple molecules of the typical elements. (Questions 7.2–7.6)

14　Given a chemical equation, write down the expression for its equilibrium constant. (Question 8.1)

15　Given the value of the equilibrium constant for a chemical reaction that seems not to occur, use it to assess what, if anything, might be done to cause the reaction to take place. (Question 8.1)

QUESTIONS: ANSWERS AND COMMENTS

Question 2.1 (Learning Outcome 2)

(a) 13; (b) 13; (c) +13e; (d) 14; (e) $^{27}_{13}$Al. Because the atomic number of aluminium is 13, there are 13 protons in the nucleus, 13 orbiting electrons in the atom, and the total charge on the nucleus is +13e. As the relative atomic mass is 27.0, and there is just one isotope, the mass number is 27. Therefore, the number of neutrons is (27 − 13) = 14. The mass number is the preceding superscript, and the atomic number is the preceding subscript in the symbol $^{27}_{13}$Al.

Question 2.2 (Learning Outcome 3)

(a) P_2O_5; (b) no. The empirical formula can be obtained from the molecular formula by reducing the ratio between the numbers of atoms to the lowest possible whole numbers. A molecule containing fewer atoms than the empirical formula would therefore consist of fractions of atoms. In chemistry, the term 'fraction of an atom' is meaningless.

Question 2.3 (Learning Outcome 4)

(a) HF is molecular; SiC is non-molecular.

(b) X is HF and Y is SiC. The chains in Figure 2.15a show that hydrogen and fluorine atoms in solid HF are separated by either a shorter distance of 92 pm or a longer distance of 157 pm. We take a hydrogen and fluorine atom separated by the shorter distance of 92 pm to be a discrete HF molecule. The shortest distance between two HF molecules is then 157 pm. In SiC, all atoms are surrounded by four others of a different type at the corners of a regular tetrahedron, the four interatomic distances being identical. There is no point at which one can stop and claim that one has reached the boundary of a molecule. SiC is therefore non-molecular. The molecular substance HF should have the lower melting and boiling temperatures, and the higher solubility in petrol. This is in fact the case.

Question 3.1 (Learning Outcome 5)

Z is tellurium (Te). The *highest* normal oxide ZO_3 suggests (point iii of Section 3.1) a highest valency of six and, therefore, a Group VI element. Point ii confirms that these elements form a hydride ZH_2. The only Group VI element that is a semi-metal is tellurium. It lies in Period 5. Its highest fluoride (point iii again) should have the empirical formula TeF_6, and in fact it does.

Question 4.1 (Learning Outcomes 6 and 7)

The elements are: (a) chlorine, Cl; (b) arsenic, As; and (c) thallium, Tl. The outer electronic configurations contain seven, five and three electrons, respectively, and are therefore characteristic of Groups VII, V and III, respectively. The principal quantum numbers of the outer electrons are three, four and six, respectively, and are equal to the Period numbers. These Group and Period numbers identify the elements when Figure 4.4 is used as a grid.

Question 4.2 (*Learning Outcomes 6 and 7*)

(a) $1s^2|2s^22p^6|3s^23p^6|4s^2$;

(b) $1s^2|2s^22p^6|3s^23p^63d^{10}|4s^24p^5$;

(c) $1s^2|2s^22p^6|3s^23p^63d^{10}|4s^24p^64d^{10}|5s^25p^2$.

With atomic numbers 20, 35 and 50, the calcium, bromine and tin atoms will contain 20, 35 and 50 electrons, respectively. Putting 20, 35 and 50 electrons into the sub-shells in the order given in Figure 4.2 yields:

(a) $1s^22s^22p^63s^23p^64s^2$;

(b) $1s^22s^22p^63s^23p^64s^23d^{10}4p^5$;

(c) $1s^22s^22p^63s^23p^64s^23d^{10}4p^65s^24d^{10}5p^2$.

Our answers are obtained from these sequences by regrouping the sub-shells in cases (b) and (c) so that they are arranged in order of increasing n value.

Question 4.3 (*Learning Outcomes 6 and 7*)

A is bismuth, Bi, and its outer electronic configuration is $6s^26p^3$. The existence of the compounds A_2O_5 and AF_5 suggests that the highest valency of A is five. This implies a Group V element. According to Figure 4.4, the only Group V element that is a metal is bismuth. As it lies in the Period 6, the outer electronic configuration of the atom is $6s^26p^3$.

Question 4.4 (*Learning Outcome 7*)

There are 17 electrons in the chlorine atom and, from Figure 4.2, the electronic configuration is $1s^22s^22p^63s^23p^5$. Turning this into a box diagram, the 1s and 2s boxes are each filled with a pair of electrons with opposite spins. The three orbitals in the 2p sub-shell and the single 3s orbital each take pairs of opposite spins in a similar way. This leaves five electrons for the three orbitals of the 3p sub-shell. We start by assigning one electron to each of the three orbitals, making sure that all three have the same spin. This maximizes the number of electrons with the same spin. The final two electrons must then go into different 3p boxes with spins opposed to the other three.

1s   2s   2p   3s   3p

Question 5.1 (*Learning Outcome 9*)

Structures **Q.1–Q.9** show the structural formulae. In each case, the number of lines issuing from each atom is equal to the element's quoted valency in Table 3.1.

H—Cl	H—N—H
	      |
	      H
		H—O
		     |
		     H
			O=O	O=C=O

Q.1	**Q.2**	**Q.3**	**Q.4**	**Q.5**

H H
| |
C=C
| |
H H

H—C≡N   H—C≡C—H

H O
| ‖
H—C—C
| |
H H

Q.6   **Q.7**   **Q.8**   **Q.9**

Question 5.2 (Learning Outcome 8)

(i) $CaCl_2$; (ii) IBr; (iii) $CaMg_2$.

The properties listed are characteristic of (i) an ionic substance, (ii) a molecular covalent substance, and (iii) a metallic substance. $CaCl_2$ is a combination of elements from the extreme left and extreme right of Figure 5.5, so the electronegativity difference will be large and $CaCl_2$ will be the ionic compound; such compounds are non-molecular. IBr will be covalent because it is a combination of elements of high electronegativity from the extreme right of Figure 5.5. $CaMg_2$ will be a metallic alloy because it is a combination of metallic elements with low electronegativity from the left of Figure 5.5. Such alloys are non-molecular.

Question 5.3 (Learning Outcome 9)

(a) For hypochlorous acid, see Structures **Q.10** and **Q.11**. The oxygen has two non-bonded pairs and two bonding pairs.

H ⚬ O ⚬ Cl

Q.10   H—O—Cl

              Q.11

(b) For SF_6, see Structures **Q.12** and **Q.13**. The sulfur atom has six bonding pairs and no non-bonded pairs.

Q.12   **Q.13**

(c) For ONCl, see Structures **Q.14** and **Q.15**. The nitrogen has one non-bonded pair and three bonding pairs.

Q.18   O=N—Cl

              Q.15

(d) For NH_2^-, the amide ion, see Structures **Q.16** and **Q.17**. The nitrogen has two bonding pairs and two non-bonded pairs.

[H ⚬ N ⚬]⁻   H—N⁻
      H   H

Q.16   **Q.17**

All the atoms in Lewis structures **Q.10**, **Q.12**, **Q.14** and **Q16** have noble gas shell structures, except for sulfur in SF_6, which is assigned twelve outer electrons.

Question 5.4 (Learning Outcome 9)

The Lewis structure of NO_3^- is shown as Structure **Q.18**. The atom of highest valency is nitrogen, so the single negative charge on the NO_3^- ion is assigned to nitrogen, giving the shell structure (2,6). All atoms gain the shell structure of neon if nitrogen forms one double bond and two single dative bonds to oxygen. Structure **Q.19** shows the two dative bonds as arrows. In the alternative representation, one of the two positive charges at the nitrogen end of the two dative bonds is cancelled by the single negative charge of the central nitrogen. This gives Structure **Q.20**.

Q.18   **Q.19**   **Q.20**

Question 5.5 (Learning Outcomes 9 and 10)

See Structures **Q.21–Q.23**.

Q.21   **Q.22**   **Q23**

In the Lewis structure **Q.21**, each bridging bromine atom forms one shared electron pair bond with one aluminium and one dative bond to the other aluminium. All atoms gain a noble gas shell structure with eight outer electrons. Structural formula **Q.22** shows the dative bonds as arrows, and suggests that the two bonds formed by each bridging bromine are different. The alternative **Q.23** makes these two bonds identical. It is therefore a better representation of the experimental data. Nevertheless, although the single formula **Q.22** is not compatible with the equal Al—Br bond lengths, this way of representing the dative bonds can be made consistent with them by using the two resonance hybrids shown in Structure **Q.24**.

Q.24

Question 5.6 (Learning Outcomes 9 and 10)

In the answer to Question 5.4, both Structure **Q.19** and Structure **Q.20** contain one double bond and two single dative bonds. Neither is therefore consistent with three equal bond lengths. To explain the discrepancy we represent the nitrate ion as the resonance hybrid shown as Structure **Q.25**.

Q.25

Question 6.1 (Learning Outcome 11)

The ethene glycol molecule contains two alcohol functional groups, —OH. These should both be replaceable by —ONO_2 groups when ethene glycol is treated with a mixture of concentrated nitric and sulfuric acids. The expected product has the structural formula **Q.26**. These expectations are correct. The product is a colourless liquid, ethene glycol dinitrate (EGDN), and it is indeed a powerful explosive.

$$CH_2-ONO_2$$
$$|$$
$$CH_2-ONO_2$$

Q.26

Question 7.1 (Learning Outcome 12)

We shall number the carbon atoms of the benzene ring from 1 to 6, calling the atom to which the —COOH or —CH$_2$COOH units are attached, carbon number 1. In Structure **7.13**, hydrogen atoms (relatively small) are attached to positions 2 and 6. Incoming reactants attacking the —COOH group attached to carbon 1 are therefore relatively unimpeded, and reaction occurs readily. In Structures **7.14** and **7.15**, the 2 and 6 positions are occupied by the much more bulky —Br and —CH$_3$ groups, respectively. These impede access of the incoming reactant to the —COOH group, thereby hindering the reaction. In Structure **7.16**, the insertion of a CH$_2$ unit between the —COOH group and carbon 1 increases the distance between the —CH$_3$ groups in positions 2 and 6 and the —COOH group. Steric hindrance is no longer severe and reaction once more occurs readily.

Question 7.2 (Learning Outcome 13)

Beryllium has two valence electrons. Both are used up in forming the two bonds to chlorine. There are two repulsion axes, so BeCl$_2$ should be linear; this is the case. Tin has four valence electrons. Two are used in forming the two single bonds to chlorine, and this leaves one non-bonded pair. There are three repulsion axes, which should therefore be disposed in a triangular sense (see Structure **Q.27**), so SnCl$_2$ should be V-shaped with a bond angle slightly less than 120° because of the primacy of the non-bonded pair–bond pair repulsions. Experimentally, this is found to be so.

Q.27

Question 7.3 (Learning Outcome 13)

(i) Nitrogen has five valence electrons, but as the NH$_4^+$ ion carries a positive charge, one must be subtracted, leaving four. All four electrons are used to form the four bonds to hydrogen, so there are just four repulsion axes, and the ion has a tetrahedral shape.

(ii) Iodine has seven valence electrons, and if one electron is added for the single negative charge on ICl$_2^-$, this becomes eight. Two of the eight electrons are used in forming single bonds to the two chlorines, leaving six which are divided into three non-bonded pairs. There are therefore five repulsion axes, which take on a trigonal-bipyramidal disposition (cf. PF$_5$, Figure 7.6d). In this arrangement, non-bonded pairs occupy equatorial positions leaving the axial positions for the two chlorines. Thus, ICl$_2^-$ is linear (Structure **Q.28**).

Q.28

(iii) Phosphorus has five valence electrons, and the negative charge of PCl$_6^-$ makes six. All six are used in forming single bonds to the six chlorines, so there are six repulsion axes: PCl$_6^-$ is octahedral like SF$_6$ in Figure 7.6e.

Question 7.4 (Learning Outcome 13)

(i) Bromine has seven valence electrons, and five of them are used to form the five Br—F bonds, leaving two as a non-bonded pair. The six repulsion axes take on an octahedral disposition, giving a square-pyramidal BrF$_5$ molecule (Structure **Q.29**). Because of the strong repulsive effect of the non-bonded pair, we would expect the angle α to be less than 90°. Experimental measurement shows this to be so (85°).

(ii) In SF$_4$, the sulfur has six valence electrons, four of which are used to form the four S—F bonds. This leaves two as a non-bonded pair. The five repulsion axes adopt the trigonal bipyramidal arrangement (Figure 7.8), with the non-bonded pair in an equatorial position. Consequently, SF$_4$ has the shape shown in Structure **Q.30**, the repulsive effect of the lone pair giving an angle β slightly less than 90°.

Q.29

Q.30

Question 7.5 (Learning Outcome 13)

(i) Sulfur has six valence electrons, and four are used up in forming two double bonds to oxygen. This leaves one non-bonded pair, giving a total of three repulsion axes. We predict a V-shaped molecule (Structure **Q.31**), with a bond angle close to 120°. The experimental value is 119.5°.

(ii) In $XeOF_4$, two of the eight xenon electrons are involved in the double bond to oxygen, and four in the Xe—F bonds, leaving one non-bonded pair. There are therefore six repulsion axes, and with four electrons assigned to the Xe=O bond, we might expect the repulsions between this bond and the non-bonded pair to be the greatest. The structure that minimizes this repulsion is the square-pyramidal **Q.32**, and this is confirmed by experiment.

Question 7.6 (Learning Outcome 13)

Nitrogen has five valence electrons and four of them will be used in forming two bonds to oxygen. This leaves a single electron. We therefore have three repulsion axes with a trigonal-planar disposition, one of them being a single electron. Structure **Q.33**, in which the nature of the N—O bonds (dative or double) is non-specific, shows this arrangment. A single non-bonded electron would be expected to exert a smaller repulsive effect than bonds or non-bonded pairs containing at least two electrons, so the angle α should be greater than 120°.
The experimentally observed value is $\alpha = 134°$.

Question 8.1 (Learning Outcomes 14 and 15)

The equilibrium constant of the first reaction, K_1, is given by

$$K_1 = \frac{[SO_3(g)]^2}{[SO_2(g)]^2[O_2(g)]}$$

That of the second, K_2 by

$$K_2 = \frac{[H_2(g)]^2[O_2(g)]}{[H_2O(g)]^2}$$

The data show that K_2 is tiny: at equilibrium, the concentrations of the hydrogen and oxygen in the numerator (the top line of the fraction) are minute in comparison with the concentration of steam in the denominator (the bottom line of the fraction). So in a closed system at 700 K, significant amounts of hydrogen and oxygen will never be formed from steam.

By contrast, K_1 is large, so the equilibrium position at 700 K lies well over to the right of the equation, and conversion of sulfur dioxide and oxygen to sulfur trioxide is favourable. The fact that the reaction does not occur must be due to a slow rate of reaction. We may therefore be able to obtain sulfur trioxide in this way if we can find a suitable catalyst to speed up the reaction. A suitable catalyst is divanadium pentoxide, V_2O_5, and at 700 K, this reaction is the key step in the manufacture of sulfuric acid from sulfur, oxygen and water. Figure 8.2 shows a similar comparison between uncatalysed and catalysed progress of reaction plots that would reflect the sulfur dioxide to sulfur trioxide conversion.

ACKNOWLEDGEMENTS

Grateful acknowledgement is made to the following sources for permission to reproduce material in this book:

Figures

Figure 2.2f: © National Power; *Figure 2.3*: Courtesy of IBM Corporation, Research Division, Almaden Research Center; *Figure 2.14*: 'Fuel hoarder sentenced', by Maurice Weaver, printed 6 April 2001, Telegraph Group Limited; *Figure 3.1*: Ann Ronan/Image Select; *Figure 5.1*: © University of California Archives; *Figure 6.2*: © ICI Nobel Explosive Co./Science Photo Library; *Figure 6.3*: © Bancroft Library, University of California; *Figure 8.3*: Johnson Matthey, Royston, Herts.

Every effort has been made to trace all the copyright owners, but if any has been inadvertently overlooked, the publishers will be pleased to make the necessary arrangements at the first opportunity.

INDEX FOR BOOKS 1 AND 2

Note Principal references are given in bold type; picture references are shown in italics. '*B1* signifies a reference in Book 1, and '*B2*' a reference in Book 2.

Rohrer, Heinrich, *B2* 38

Rutherford model of atom, *B2* 36, 53

S

salt; *see* sodium chloride

saturated hydrocarbon, *B2* **79**

scanning tunnelling microscopy, *B2* 38

Semtex, *B2* 80

sialidase, *B1* 18

silica; *see* silicon dioxide

silicon, electronic configuration of, *B2* 54–5, 58

silicon carbide, structure of, *B2* 47

silicon dioxide (silica, quartz), *B1* 9; *B2* 43, 45, 67

SLIMDIS (liquid crystal display), *B1* 15

sodium, *B2 37*

sodium chloride (common salt), *B2* 40, 42–3, 45, 63–4

space-filling models, *B1 10*; *B2 82*, 83

spin (electronic), *B2* **58**, 60–1

square-planar coordination, *B2* **89**

SQUIDs (superconducting quantum interference devices), *B1* 21

StarOffice, *B1* 30

state symbols, *B2* 70

steric effects, *B2* **84**

structural formulae, *B2* **66**

    condensed, *B2* 76

Study File, *B1* 29–30

substrate of enzyme action, *B2* 84

sulfur, *B2* 37

sulfur hexafluoride, *B2* 85, 86

superconductors, *B1* 20–1

symbols; *see* chemical symbols

synthetic materials, *B1* 10

T

television sets, flat-screen, *B1* 15

tetrafluoromethane, *B2* 85

tetrahedral coordination, *B2* **85**

thermometer, liquid crystal display for, *B1 15*

thionyl chloride, reaction of, with alcohols, *B2* 76, 77

three-way catalytic converter, *B2* 96, *97*, *98*

tin oxide, empirical formula of, *B2* 50

TNT, *B2* 80

transition elements, electronic configurations of, *B2* 55

trigonal bipyramidal coordination, *B2* **86**, 90

trigonal planar coordination, *B2* **85**

2,4,6-trinitrophenol (picric acid), *B2* 79, 80

typical elements, *B2* 48, 52, 57–8

V

valence-shell electron-pair repulsion theory (VSEPR theory), *B2* **87**–90

valency, *B2* 50, 51

vibrational spectra, *B2* 67

VSEPR theory (valence-shell electron-pair repulsion theory), *B2* 87–90

W

water

    Lewis structure for, *B2* 68

    molecular shape of, *B2* 86–7, 89

WebLab ViewerLite, *B1* 30

X

xenon tetrafluoride, molecular shape of, *B2* 87–9

Y

YBCO (superconductor), *B1* 20, *21*